By the end of the first half, the two teams wer
handed, as the score was tied at 0-0. As the
the second half, the voices of their coaches
heads. Just six minutes into the second half
game drew open its curtain.

It began with a pass to the Argentine football magician, Diego Mara
England's half of the pitch. With the ball glued to Maradona's lethal left foot, the English players could see the dark pillars of cloud gathering.

The English defenders buzzed after him like flies, hoping to intercept the ball. A look at the English stand would expose the fear that blared in their eyes. They knew that a ball glued to Maradona's left foot around the 18-yard box never stumbles out until it kisses the net. As the English defenders built roadblocks around the magician, he cut through them with acute twists and turns.

Sighting his teammate Jorge Valdano, who was already waiting for a pass, he passed the ball to him and made a run for a true pass. Jorge was trying to get control of the ball when Steve Hodge, the English side midfielder, mistakenly looped the ball high in the air towards their goalpost in a desperate rush to get the ball out, making it a contest between their on-rushing keeper Peter Shilton and Maradona.

With a height difference of about 20 centimeters between Peter and Maradona, the hearts of the English players had a momentary rest, knowing that Peter had a massive chance of getting to the ball first before Maradona. Although Maradona knew he had less chance of getting to the ball, he still took a jump of faith into the air in an aerial battle with Peter.

Before Peter could lay claim to the ball, in a split-second act that escaped the eyes of the referee and the linesmen, Maradona punched the ball with his left hand, putting it right into the net. It was a goal. A goal that birthed the famous football slang, "Hand of God".

This moment of cheeky play inscribed his name in the hearts of his compatriots. It was a goal that set them on the path to lifting the World Cup in the tournament. It was the year that made Maradona a name that rang a bell worldwide.

However, before Maradona leaped into the limelight of the world's most loved sport, he was a boy growing up in the neighborhood of Villa Fiorito on the outskirts of Argentina's capital, Buenos Aires. With houses built with scrap metal sheets and wood spread like scarecrows on its muddy street, Villa Fiorito had every weapon to kill the dream of the football legend who would make a powerful impact on the world of football.

Born on October 30, 1960, as the fifth child to a factory worker father, Diego Maradona Senior, and his mother, Dalma Salvadora Franco, who poured her heart into the care of her small home. Maradona did not wake up in a cradle filled with roses; the sunset of financial struggles cast a shadow of lack into their home.

However, even with a poorly lit chandelier of hard life hanging relatively low in Villa Fiorito, Maradona still found a way to squeeze joy out of its rocks. With a father who played football recreationally, it was not difficult for the young Maradona to fall in love with the sport that kept his young feet busy. So, together with his friends, they turned the dusty streets of Villa Fiorito into their field.

One would think that with the passion and excitement with which Maradona played with his friends on the streets, they kicked real football. If you think so, you might be stretching your imagination too far for the little kids of Villa Fiorito.

Maradona's family could not afford to buy him an actual football. However, the talent and passion that rustled through his bones were quite impatient in waiting for things to improve so his family could afford a ball.

So, together with his friends, they improvised. They made rags into balls and played the rag ball barefooted on the sunbaked rough streets of Villa Fiorito, their excitement sending peals of laughter echoing in the neighborhood as though it mocked it for its inability to snatch their joy.

Inspirational Sports Stories for Kids

Captivating Tales of How 15 Sports Legends Rose to Greatness, That Will Inspire Young Athletes to Build Mental Toughness to Overcome Challenges.

BY

Michael Chuku

TABLE OF CONTENTS

INTRODUCTION

Imagine a young athlete entering the arena full of potential but facing a formidable opponent or a challenging situation, like missing the last shot in a basketball game, losing a race by seconds, or falling short in a competition. The disappointment can be overwhelming. Without mental toughness, these setbacks can crush their confidence, making them question their abilities and even give up on their dreams.

The pressure to perform, the fear of failure, and the weight of expectations can become too much to bear. For many young athletes, not being mentally prepared means losing more than just a game: it can mean losing their passion and drive to succeed.

But what if you could flip the script? **What if your kid could take on challenges with a mindset that says, "YES I CAN!"?** Diego Maradona, for instance, began his journey playing soccer with a ball made of rags on the dusty streets of Villa Fiorito, Argentina. With limited resources, he focused on developing his skills, turning those humble beginnings into a legendary career.

Similarly, Jerry Rice, who caught bricks at his construction job, transformed this experience into exceptional hand-eye coordination, becoming one of the greatest football receivers of all time. With the right mindset, even the toughest challenges become stepping stones to greatness.

"Inspirational Sports Stories for Kids" is packed with tales that show how 15 sports legends didn't just overcome setbacks; they crushed them through passion, hard work, and mental toughness.

How does just reading stories help my kid develop mental strength? You may ask!

According to research from the American Psychological Association, kids who learn about overcoming challenges are more likely to persist in the face of their obstacles. Another study from Stanford University found that understanding others' struggles can foster a growth mindset, helping kids believe they can improve with effort and perseverance.

This book isn't just about sports; it's about life. Kids will be entertained by fun, action-packed stories while learning valuable lessons. They will discover how LeBron James became the youngest player to score 20,000 career points and get inspired by athletes like Simone Biles and Novak Djokovic, who turned their challenges into victories.

With every page, kids will uncover quotes that motivate them to keep pushing forward, like, "I'm not the next Usain Bolt or Michael Phelps. I'm the Simone Biles."

Kids experience challenges every day. Each day, kids go without being mentally tough; they risk encountering a challenge that may **break** them mentally, which may cause you more time and money to fix.

Reading inspiring stories in this book is a simple and effective way to help young minds build the mental strength to turn setbacks into comebacks, both in sports and life. **So, dive in now and start reading these heroic stories with exciting twists and turns!**

DIEGO MARADONA

The first half of the match was a test of strength: even the glazing teeth of the hot summer sun didn't have enough bite force to sink its teeth into the muscled bodies of the twenty-two men, bleeding with sweat and passion for their country, as they ran round the football pitch of Azteca Stadium.

It was not just a battle of honor for the country; it was a battle of ego between two elephants in the most loved sports in the world.

The year was 1986, in Mexico City. It was the World Cup quarter-final match between Argentina and England. With a crowd of about 100,000 fans taking every space with booming loud cheers, silence had no place in the stadium.

Maradona's first taste of a real ball came when his uncle gifted him an old, worn-out football. This was the best gift he had received in his young life. He didn't let the ball out of his sight. He cherished it so much and would sleep beside it every night. The football condition didn't matter to him because, for the first time, he and his friends would have the opportunity to play real football.

This gift boosted his passion. As he grew, fishing his joys from his sole passion, football, his skills began to flower. He would practice for hours every day. His practice routine included dribbling the ball around rocks and other obstacles. With each touch, he transformed the streets into his stadium, where every kick was a step toward his destiny.

His exceptional ball control, which made it seem the ball was always glued to his feet, and his swift, flexible movements, which made it easy for him to skillfully meander through a defense, showed him to be miles ahead of his peers and announced him to the neighborhood of Villa Fiorito.

With relentless hard work, determination, and discipline that didn't wait for the world to be okay before he could pursue his dreams, Maradona leaves an invaluable lesson: we must start chasing our dreams from our little spaces with things available to us. And maybe, one day, our hard work will meet with opportunity.

On a Saturday afternoon in March 1969, in Saavedra Park, a neighborhood of Buenos Aires, Maradona's hard work walked into the open doors of opportunity. While weaving his feet around the ball in its dusty soccer field, his magnetic skills caught the keen eyes of Francis Cornejo, the coach of a local youth football team, Los Cebollitas.

Watching the eight-year-old's incredible skill pressed the push button of Coach Francis's mouth, and his jaw dropped in amazement. When Maradona told him his age, he didn't believe him. The magic skills were just too large to fit into the tiny, short legs of the young lad.

Confident he had found a star, Coach Francis invited the eight-year-old Maradona to join Los Cebollitas, the youth team of Argentinos Juniors. Under the keen guidance of Coach Francis, Maradona's exceptional skills and natural ability on the ball began to blossom.

Maradona's incredible performances at Los Cebollitas would have sounded unbelievable if it had happened in a fairy tale. With his presence in the team, they went on a streak of one hundred and thirty-six games without a loss.

This impressive stat would make one think it came on a platter without challenges. The truth is that his time at Argentinos Juniors was challenging. His exceptional talent and skills were a ladder, and the pressure of expectations walked onto his young shoulders, heaping the burden of immense scrutiny. However, his family's support and relentless dedication to improving himself eased the burden of the pressure.

Having shone a floodlight of complete dominance in the junior team, the young Maradona walked into senior football in 1976. His professional debut came on October 20, 1976, ten days before his 16th birthday.

Coach Francis Cornejo, who has been with him since discovering him, knew that the young Maradona might get overwhelmed playing in a team where he was the youngest. So, he said to him, "Keep the ball close to your feet, trust your instincts, and always play with joy." The words of Maradona's coach were an endless music playing in his head.

After dazzling fans at Argentinos Juniors for almost a decade, Maradona's talent hungered for a new environment to ply his trade. In 1981, he joined Boca Juniors, one of Argentina's most prestigious clubs. Despite offers from European teams, Maradona's heart was set on playing for Boca.

His debut on February 22, 1981, was nothing short of magical. Wearing the iconic blue and yellow jersey, he scored twice against Talleres de Córdoba, leading Boca to a 4-1 victory. A win with which he announced his presence.

Pressure and high expectations were faithful shadows that followed Maradona everywhere. It came along with him to Boca. Despite winning the Metropolitano championship in 1981, he faced intense media scrutiny and the pressure of high expectations. Yet, his resilience shone through, and he continued mesmerizing football fans with his skills.

1982 walked Maradona out of the shores of Argentina. Pushed by passion, he made a significant move to FC Barcelona in Spain for a world-record transfer fee. One of his iconic moments came in the 1983 Copa del Rey final, where he scored and led Barcelona to a 2-1 victory over Real Madrid. In just two seasons, Maradona scored 38 goals in 58 matches he played at Barcelona.

However, Maradona's journey in FC Barcelona was not smooth. In September 1983, a reckless tackle from Andoni Goikoetxea of Athletic Bilbao handed him a severe ankle injury. The injury took him captive for months and starved him of his passion for months. It was sheer perseverance and determination that nursed him back, pushing him to bounce back to his top form.

Maradona climbed to the peak of his career in 1984. Transferring to Napoli in Italy was a move that would cement his legendary status. Leading the team to their first-ever Serie A title in 1987, a UEFA Cup in 1989, and another Serie A title in 1990, he made his name a song that played in the hearts of every football lover in the city.

With a mountain of success he planted in clubs, Maradona poured the same energy into his country. On June 29, 1986, he led Argentina to a World Cup final against West Germany. With the match tied at 2-2 in the 80th minute, Maradona, in a rare moment of exceptional brilliance, made a through pass to Jorge Burruchaga, who sealed the game in the 84th minute, dragging the Argentines to a 3-2 win: a win that testifies to his unusual brilliance and passion for his country.

Sadly, the evening of his career in Spain in the 1980s, when he got involved with drugs, cast a long shadow that almost wiped out his legendary footprints due to his abuse of drugs. In 1991, Maradona was slammed with a 15-month suspension after testing positive for cocaine. The 1994 World Cup saw him handed another high-profile suspension for testing positive for ephedrine.

Maradona's involvement with drugs was the heavy rain that drenched the fire of his impressive skills, sent him thunderstorms of injuries, and crippled the engine of his illustrious career in 1997 when he retired. It is a lesson that our actions have consequences. In his illustrious career, he played four World Cups and scored 34 goals in 91 international appearances for Argentina.

However, these lessons stand on the back of Maradona's impressive career: Passion is the fuel on which the car of success runs. Secondly, an opportunity never gives one time to prepare. Thirdly, it takes one bad habit to cripple years of hard work.

Speak your Mind

When you don't have everything you need for a project or a game, like the perfect supplies or equipment, how do you think you can still get things done?

Can you think of a time when you had to use your imagination or work extra hard because you didn't have all the tools you wanted? What unique skills did you develop by being creative in those situations?

Making the Most Out of Little

When resources are limited, being creative and thinking outside the box is essential. For example, legendary soccer player Diego Maradona began his journey by making a football out of rags and playing on the streets. He didn't have fancy equipment or a big field, but he used what he had and made the most of it. This resourcefulness helped him develop incredible skills that led to a successful career.

LEBRON JAMES

It was not fear that pulled the buttocks of the Cleaveland Cavaliers' fans off their seats on the evening of Sunday, 16th June 2016, during the NBA final game against the Golden State Warriors at the Oracle Arena.

It was hunger. A desperate hunger for the NBA championship title, which they have been starved of for the past fifty-two years. The final 3 minutes 39 seconds of the fourth quarter, was stretched as both teams held on tightly, unwilling to give the other a chance.

A peek into the arena would find the Cavalier fans standing as though they wouldn't forgive themselves if their eyes missed a moment of the game. While they stood, one would have expected that with the scoreline tied in matching jerseys of 89-89 and with the cloud of uncertainty looming, their lips would be shut to prevent the loud drums of their pounding hearts from breaking out of their mouths.

Instead, their lips were busy with a chant of the name of a maestro, their 6'9-foot Cleaveland homeboy, on whose giant shoulders they have rode to the moment. His name is LeBron James.

LeBron's history with his home team, the Cavaliers, is a bittersweet love affair. This love burned in the hearts of the fans tonight as they watched a sweaty LeBron in their NBA finals against the favorite Golden State Warriors. So far, it has been a tough match, with the Warriors taking the lead in the first and second quarters. The third quarter saw LeBron James pulling the Cavaliers back to the top.

Now, with 1:51 seconds remaining in the fourth quarter, dark clouds began to gather at the court. The Warriors' Andre Iguodala, fed with a fastbreak, swiftly moves to their loop. With a tie score at 89, the fastbreak would seal the game.

Anxiety moistened the eyes of the Cavalier's fans. The thought of losing yet another final gave them a panic attack. Even the giant strides of LeBron sprinting down the court in a chase-down seemed hopeless. Before LeBron arrived, Andre was already in midair, detaching his hand from the ball for a short. It was almost too late for a save.

Then, in a flash, like a thunderbolt, a stunning moment that redefined the game miraculously appeared. LeBron's windmill arm stretched and gave a thunderous block to the ball, replanting hope in the hearts of the Cavaliers.

Even though the Golden State Warriors fans filled most of the arena, LeBron's incredible save made the crowd feel like it was all about him. The Cavaliers' cheers for 'King James' were so loud they drowned out the Warriors' home crowd.

Before we dive into the thrilling final moments of this game, let's first take a journey back to where it all began for LeBron James: a story that revolves entirely around "King James", just like the Cavaliers fans' cheers.

In the heart of Akron, Ohio, where the streets weave stories of resilience and hope, a star was born on December 30, 1984. This star was LeBron James, arriving in the world to a sixteen-year-old mother, Gloria Marie James. With his father, Anthony McClelland, absent, Gloria had to shoulder the heavy burden of parenthood alone amidst the challenges of their environment.

From birth, life already gave LeBron enough on his plate to even think of basketball. With poverty hanging like a broken chandelier on his family's neck, LeBron was forced to continually move around with his family as they fished through different poor neighborhoods in Akron, looking for a place to lay their heads and live their lives.

At this point, LeBron's dream was survival, not basketball. With many vices feasting in the clouds of Akron's poor neighborhoods, it was difficult for a young boy of LeBron's age to survive without catching the virus.

At age nine, it took a stroke of luck for a dream other than survival to find space in his troubled heart. During this time, he moved in with Frank Walker, a basketball coach. The coach introduced him to the world of basketball.

A new LeBron emerged with a blood of new passion running in his veins. It didn't take long before his talent unraveled. Later on, Walker introduced him to the local leagues, where he became a floodlight, shining brightly. In 1999, at 15, his light bled into the eyes of St. Vincent-St. Mary High School, who recruited him to join their team.

As a freshman in the high school team, LeBron held onto the team like a drowning man, grabbing everything that came his way. By the end of Junior year, he had pulled the team by their bootstraps to claim two State Division III titles, earned a place in the USA Today All-USA First Team, and was named the Gatorade Player of the Year and the Parade Magazine High School Basketball Player of the Year. LeBron's impressive record was so towering that recruiters began scrambling for him right after his junior year.

This was the first challenge LeBron faced in his career. He was torn between going pro and finishing high school. Given his poor background, going pro held a strong appeal, as it would not only give him and his family a better life but also give him an edge. On the other hand, finishing high school would help him finish his education and help his team, who were the first to give him a chance at the fame he now enjoys.

LeBron decided to finish high school. A decision that spread a large grin on the face of his high school. In senior year, LeBron was a lion whose roar claimed the court. He had an incredible record that pulled his team to pocket the state's Division III Championship title for the third time, placing them at the top of the national ranking. By the end of his high school career, LeBron had amassed a mouth-watering stat of 2,657 points, 892 rebounds, and 523 assists.

Having decided to go pro instead of college, with a career stat that stretched beyond the borders of Ohio State, LeBron was a lamplight that gathered moths of recruiters all over the country.

So, in the 2003 NBA Draft, 19-year-old LeBron was the first pick for the Cleaveland Cavaliers, who signed the young, talented forward. It was here that the bittersweet relationship between LeBron and the Cavaliers started.

The Cavaliers were a struggling side. Their standing in the Eastern Conference in the last season was eighth place. However, when LeBron walked into the 2003-2004 season, he was like the light at the end of the tunnel for the Cavaliers. He became a bundle of energy that sowed hope in his teammates on the court.

They rode on the back of his excellence as he averaged 20 points per game. His impressive run in the season earned him the NBA Rookie of the Year Award at the age of 20. It was the first of its kind in the Cavalier franchise.

However, a hunger opened up in the heart of LeBron. It was the hunger for the NBA Championship title. After several attempts in 2006, he burnt sweat and blood to pull the Cavaliers to the NBA finals. Unfortunately, they lost their championship bid by losing to the San Antonio Spurs in four consecutive games.

This did not quench LeBron's hunger. With the blows life has dealt him, giving up was not a trait he had. In the following season, he pushed again, leading the Cavaliers up the standings in the Eastern Conference. This time, the team reached the semifinals of the NBA Championship. However, they lost to the Boston Celtics in seven games.

As the 2008-2009 NBA season unfolded, tension began to brew between LeBron James and the Cleveland Cavaliers. With LeBron's contract nearing its end, rumors about his future swirled. Fans hoped he'd stay to deliver the NBA Championship that had eluded them for over four decades. LeBron, aware of these high expectations, consistently downplayed the speculation, focusing on winning with his current team. But by the season's end, LeBron made the shocking decision to join the Miami Heat, leaving Cleveland fans devastated.

The reaction was intense. In the streets of Cleveland, angry fans burned replicas of his jersey, and hate speeches flooded the air. Dan Gilbert, the majority owner of the Cleaveland Cavalier, described LeBron's decision in an open letter as "selfish, heartless, and a cowardly betrayal."

This marked the end of the lovebird's relationship. Despite the pressure that came and the emotional blackmail that trailed his decisions, he stuck to his guns. He knew that to help the Cavalier, he needed to be strong; otherwise, they would both sink. LeBron's decision is a lesson that we might sometimes have to make hard decisions in our journey. Although it may not be favorable to everyone, we must do what feels true.

The Miami sky had many stars for LeBron to pluck. After an impressive first season, the 2011-2012 season gave him the very title his heart has yearned for so long. In the fifth game in the NBA finals against the Oklahoma City Thunder, LeBron did not shy away from showing, with his excellent display, that he desperately needed the title.

In the game, he made 26 points, 11 rebounds, and 13 assists to clinch the title whose quest dragged him out of Cavalier. After the match, the overly excited LeBron said, "I made a difficult decision to leave Cleaveland, but I understood what my future was about. I knew we had a bright future in Miami."

Success broke its rain on LeBron in the 2012-2013 season. First, he made his 20,000 career points to become the youngest player and the 38th player in NBA history to achieve such a feat. Secondly, he won his second NBA Championship title.

A third title almost followed in the 2012-14 season during the NBA finals against San Antonio; however, they lost after five games. With an impressive run at the Miami Heat, LeBron was an eye candy in the NBA world. Everyone wanted him.

However, with his quest for the championship title quenched. LeBron knew he now had the armory of experience and skill he needed to fulfill his promise to the Cleaveland. Keeping to his word, he opted out of his contract with the Miami Heat. Even with the hands of other teams pulling him to their side, his eyes were set homewards.

The 2014-2015 season saw LeBron reunited with his first love, The Cavaliers. A move that burst the bad blood that existed between them. From here, LeBron's life and career journey launched us back to the 16th of June 2016 NBA final game that started his story.

With 53 seconds left, Cavalier's Irving found the loop with a three-point shot, giving the team the lead. The scoreline of 89-92 saw the Cavaliers defending with their lives. However, the Warriors still managed a pass that caught the fiery hands of Curry, who swiftly took a 3-point shot. It was a miss that LeBron pounced on to lead the final attack against the Warriors.

The chorus, "King James! King James!" ate up the oracle arena as LeBron attempted a kill layup. A foul denied the Cavaliers the point and offered them a free throw. After a miss of the first shot, LeBron could hear the heavily pounding heartbeats of the Cavalier fans.

He didn't disappoint. He scored. Before they could run down their court half for defense, the buzzer went off. Cavalier has broken the 52-year-old jinx. LeBron was drowned in a river of hugs by the crowd of fans who broke into the court with moist eyes to thank him.

An emotional LeBron broke down in tears. In a post-match interview, LeBron, in an emotionally drenched voice, said, "I came back to bring a championship to our city. I knew what I was capable of doing. I knew what I learned in the last couple of years that I was gone, and I knew if I had to win when I came back- I knew I had the right ingredients and the right blueprint to help this franchise get back to a place that we've never been".

With his promise kept, LeBron went on to stay at the Cavalier's side, dragging them up the Eastern Conference standings and leading them to the NBA finals. On July 1, 2018, when he announced his next career move to the Los Angeles Lakers, the Cavalier fans, happy that he had kept his word to them and given them his very best, bade him a good farewell.

The face of LeBron's first season with the Lakers broke no smile. A back and knee injury, and later a groin injury, kept him out of play for most of the season. This affected the Lakers' play, who were hoping for the Maestro's impact.

However, the next season, LeBron came with magnetic gloves, setting impressive records and claiming every title his wide arms could reach. At 39, he is the NBA's leading scorer and has won almost everything to be won in the game.

The hallmark of LeBron's inspiring story is a true testament that you have no excuses not to succeed.

Speak your Mind

Can you think of a time when you felt pressure to do well in school, sports, or another activity because others were counting on you?

How did that make you feel: Proud or Nervous?

How did you deal with it, and what could you do differently next time?

Handling the Pressure of Expectations

LeBron was labeled as "The Chosen One" in high school, with enormous expectations placed on him. Despite the pressure, he remained committed to **improving his skills**, leading him to become one of the greatest basketball players of all time.

It is important to embrace high expectations and use them as motivation rather than being overwhelmed by them. Don't let pride stop you from improving yourself, and don't let fear of failing to limit you from taking risks.

CRISTIANO RONALDO

Of all the things that could make your heart run into a panic while watching the UEFA Champions League final between Chelsea FC and Manchester United on May 21, 2008, it was not the presence of Cristiano Ronaldo standing before a spot kick in the night that would hand him his first UEFA championship league title.

For someone who carried the United team throughout the group stage of the tournament up to the night's final in the Luzhniki Stadium, Moscow, Russia, where his 26th-minute header in the first half slipped past Petre Cech, giving the Red Devils a lead that would later be equalized, it was surprising that Ronaldo standing before the spot kick made the hearts of the excited United fans jittery.

With the casual confidence of one who had seen the end of the match from the beginning, the 23-year-old star standing a 10-yard distance from the set ball before the intimidating gaze of Petre Cech wasn't scared when the whistle announced that it was time he did the needful. Ronaldo was sure that the ball would be perfectly buried behind the net in the next five seconds. With eyes fixed on Cech, he took his stuttering run, his signature approach in penalty shootouts, and then it came.

A thunder strike of low-level range shot fired with his monster power parked right foot towards the right side of the goal post. It was going to be a goal until Cech lunged after the ball with the vengeance of one who once beaten was twice shy. He punched the ball out.

The Wing of the Manchester fan base went silent. A crackling sound of something breaking slipped into the silence. It was Ronaldo's heart. A tsunami of emotions quaked his metal frame. His miss had automatically handed Chelsea FC a chance to take the championship title. The thought of being remembered as the guy who gave away the title with his kick hit him hard.

Although the United in a twist of fate, stole a 6-5 win against Chelsea, with a save from Van der Sar, Ronaldo knew there was work to do. In the evening of the next day, while his teammates were resting, Ronaldo went to training. A testament to the metallic strength of his will, insane work ethic, and incredible passion for the game of football on whose wings he had flown to succeed against all odds.

Born on the 5th of February 1985, under the malnourished clouds of a small island in Funchal, Madeira, Portugal, as the last child of a family of four, to a father who had a good relationship with alcohol and a mother, whose hands were busy as a cook and a cleaner, life already dealt Cristiano Ronaldo dos Santos Aveiro with the wrong card at birth.

Although his early life was pebbled with the scowling face of hardship, his mind had enough room to let in the light of his passion. His interest in soccer was kindled by his dad who worked as an equipment manager for Andorina, a boy's club. This was all the fuel that Ronaldo needed to become a wildfire. His life was rolled into a ball of hunger for football. It was here that his football career began, at age five.

At age 10, the lanky lad had become a major sensation in the neighborhood. Everyone knew him as the boy whose breath stank of football. His godfather, Fernao Sousa, while commenting on Ronaldo's passion in an interview with British reporters, said: "All he wanted to do as a child was play football. He loved the game so much he'd miss meals or escape out of his bedroom window with a ball when he was supposed to be doing homework".

Although Ronaldo was a popular boy in school, he didn't like school. So, at age 14, with his reputation as a prodigy in the world of football sweeping through his hometown and drawing the attention of the local clubs, following a discussion with his mother, he decided to quit schooling and focus on his career. It was this decision that rolled his first dice in football.

The sky of Ronaldo's dream got gloomy at 15 when he was diagnosed with tachycardia. A rare heart condition that made his heart beat much faster than normal. He needed urgent surgery. Both Ronaldo and his mum feared the worst: scared that the surgery would deny Ronaldo his chance of ever playing football. But a few days after a successful surgery the young Ronaldo was at the pitch training

With legs burdened by the restlessness of passion, he went ahead to play for Clube Desportivo Nacional of Madeira and later on to Sporting Lisbon until 2003 when the major daybreak of his career arrived. It was on the night of August 6, in a preseason friendly match between Lisbon and Manchester United at the opening of the Jose Alvavade stadium.

At that time, no one knew the 18-year-old Ronaldo beyond the shores of Portugal. It would be the first real match he'd play against one of the biggest clubs in Europe. Ronaldo was scared, but he knew this was also an opportunity to launch himself into the eyes of the world. So, as soon as the whistle pressed the start button, Ronaldo became a wildfire that ate up the stadium.

Wearing Jersey No. 28, he fearlessly rained fire and brimstone on the Manchester United defense, as though he had a grudge against them, especially the right back, John O'Shea, whom he turned into a little puppy in the field, making him chase him endlessly, even while he kept bombarding him with his stepovers and sprints that pulled spinning strings that left migraine sounds in his head. At halftime, with Ronaldo tearing down the wall of the Red Devils' defense, Lisbon had a goal lead.

Recalling this historic moment in his autobiography, Roy Keane, former United captain said: "I saw how good Ronaldo was that day. He was up against John O'Shea. Sheasy ended up seeing a doctor at halftime because he was having dizzy spells." In the second half of the game, Ronaldo was a volcano that O'Shea could not tame. In the 53rd minute of the game, another player came to take his place.

If one had spared a look at the face of Alex Ferguson, United's coach, as Ronaldo molded his players into folding chairs, one would not only see the fascination but the hopeful smile of one who had chanced on a lucky charm. By the time the whistle, put an end to the suffering of the United defense on the 90th minute, Lisbon had won the game with a three-goal lead to a measly one by the European giant.

After the match, the hands of Alex Ferguson became grabby. He knew that if Ronaldo stepped out of that stadium that night with the magic wand his legs waved, he would lose him. So, he began talking with him immediately. Ten days after the night of the magic in Lisbon, in a record signing of 12 million pounds, which made him the most expensive signing in the English premier league then, Ronaldo made his debut for United in a match against Bolton. Stepping into Old Trafford, Ronaldo knew he was standing on the scaffolds of hope, there was little room for disappointment. He lived up to his promise.

He was a bloodthirsty predator, preying on the opponent's defense with his trademark dizzying stepovers that invoked a rain of migraines on the defense, and his sprints that made defenders board buses in pursuit. He became the very heartbeat of the United team. His punitive style of play and his boundless energy made him the real devil of the Red Devils

However, it wasn't all rosy for the Portuguese star during his spell at Old Trafford. A roller-coaster of hard emotions ran through him in 2005, when he lost his dad to kidney problems induced by his long drinking habits. With the role his father played in his footballing career, the news was a red-hot iron that drove into his soul.

Also, the 2006/2007 season, saw Ronaldo earning a lorry load of boos from the English fans. Their immense love for him was brewed into hate by an incident that took place in the 2006 quarter-final match between Portugal and England at Gelsenkirchen, Germany. The England Star-studded team, which had the likes of Wayne Rooney, his teammate, was the favorite to win the match.

Unfortunately, in the 61st minute of the game still met the English team with no goal. Then a rough tackle and stamping on Ricardo Carvalho by a frustrated Rooney, an act of revenge for an earlier fouling by Ricardo which had gone unnoticed by the referee, bagged Rooney a red card.

But the drama had come before the red card, when the English players hovered over Horacio Elizondo, the referee, pleading the cause of Rooney, while Ronaldo was everywhere in front of the Referee, protesting that Rooney be sent out.

Rooney's match out of the field was followed by a cheeky wink from Ronaldo. This didn't sit well with the English fans who saw it as a betrayal on the part of Ronaldo. They held onto the grudge and carried it back to England. They believed Rooney being sent off the pitch had cost them the tournament.

Portugal went ahead to win the match in a 3-1 lead, with a decisive kick from Ronaldo.

Even with a thinned admiration of the fans, Ronaldo didn't sulk. He doubled on his efforts. And soon, the hands of hate of the fans became too small to shield the echo of his impressive performances. Soon, like early rains, their love for him reappeared. This act of Ronaldo teaches an invaluable lesson: focus on your goals and don't chase the applause.

In 2008, at 23, after an approximately six-year spell in the Man United team, he became the best player in the EPL. He had a large appetite. He took everything. With his 292 appearances, he cemented his name in the club by winning the Champions League title, three Premier League titles, two league cups, the FA Cup, the club World Cup and pocketing 118 goals. Finally, he claimed the highest honor in football by winning his first Ballon d'Or.

After an impressive season with the Red Devils, in 2009, 24-year-old Ronaldo bowed out and joined the Spanish giants, Real Madrid, in a world record transfer fee of $131 million. With that insane amount, Ronaldo knew it wouldn't be a walk in the park. A mountain of pressure sat on his shoulder. In his words: "I know that they are going to demand a lot from me to be successful at the club and I know that I'm going to have much more pressure than at Manchester United…But it means a new challenge and is going to help me be the best footballer."

True to his words, Real Madrid became the hearth where he was forged into a beast. It was a major turning point in his career. He conquered the Spanish league. In almost a decade at the Spanish giants club, he led Real Madrid to claim four UEFA Champions League titles, bagged 450 goals, four Ballon d'Or, to tie the mark of his foremost rival Lionel Messi, and additional individual awards from UEFA and France Football Magazine.

Apart from club football, Ronaldo was the very backbone of his country's football team. As the captain, he was the team's reservoir of hope. Speaking on his influence, his teammates said, "He gave us a lot of confidence". One such day was the night was the 10th of July 2016, after a hard-fought run in the

European Championship he single-handedly hurled his team to the final against France.

The outcome of the night was obvious. With France being the much stronger team, the night was to be a walk in the park. Twenty-five minutes into the first half, the hearts of the Portuguese players and their fans broke. Ronaldo was injured and hurled off the pitch. With the team's engine gone, they became a broken vehicle. But it was not long before a limping Ronaldo began walking the length and breadth of the pitch with a syringe. Injecting faith and courage into his teammates.

By the time, the referee's whistle gripped the legs of the frustrated French players to a stop, the legs of the Portuguese players had run wild in excitement. It was a 1-0 win in their favor. They have landed their first international trophy. It was an emotional victory. If one had stared deep into Ronaldo's chest, one would have seen his heart restless in excitement.

Speaking to the press after the match, overwhelmed Ronaldo said, "This is one of the happiest moments in my career". Unfortunately, the 2018 and 2022, World Cup tournaments, did not have Ronaldo in their good books. Despite his impressive runs, Portugal was bullied out in the tournaments at the knockout stages. In all, he would score a total of 131 goals for the Portuguese team.

Meanwhile, back in Real Madrid, Ronaldo was already hungry for a new challenge. So, his career took a new trajectory in July 2018, when he joined the Italian Giants, Juventus, for a record fee of $140 million. From there, in August 2021, he headed back to the very club that made his name music in the soul of professional football: Manchester United.

However, in November 2022, barely a year after his return, he ended things with the club due to a frosty relationship that brewed between them. On December 30, 2022, he moved to Al-Nasser, a Saudi league, in a three-year mind-blowing contract that was worth $200 million.

At 39, Ronaldo's boots are still perfectly laced in his feet. Although his whirlwind sprints and dizzying dribbles have thinned, his passion and unbreakable will seem to have no expiring dates.

On September 5, 2024, Ronaldo made history in the world of football. In a UEFA Nations League 2-1 win over Croatia, he became the first-ever male player to score 900 career goals across all competitions. Even at this, he has no plans of stopping.

Arguments might continue to arise about the best player in the world, however, no one can take away the fact that Ronaldo remains the most prolific goal scorer in the world. Despite the bad press that always came on his heels at the slightest turn, which made him out as an overwhelmingly arrogant individual, and having had to continually prove himself, as he was always compared with his Argentine rival, Lionel Messi, Ronaldo didn't cower to the pressures.

He stood up for himself and with sheer hard work, nailed himself to the spotlight. In all, Ronaldo's life leaves an invaluable lesson, to succeed at anything, hard work, passion, confidence, and strong will are the three things that must be on the menu.

Speak your Mind

How do you think you can grow your skills and talent by having fun while staying resilient? For example, basketball players like Stephen Curry made drills fun to improve shooting, and swimmers like Katie Ledecky used music during training to stay motivated. Cristiano Ronaldo found joy in creative footwork challenges to sharpen his skills.

How do you think making practice fun can help you stay strong and chase your dreams when things get tough?

Fun Ways to Boost Talent and Strengthen Resilience

Growing your talent and building resilience can be exciting if you make it fun! To improve, try turning your practice into creative games. Set small challenges for yourself, like making a fun goal during practice or timing how fast you can complete drills. Use your imagination to invent new moves or try different tricks with your equipment.

Staying positive and playful, even when things get tough, will help you bounce back quicker from mistakes. Invite your friends to join in, and celebrate each other's progress. Most importantly, enjoy every step of learning. When you're having fun, you'll grow faster and stronger without even noticing!

NAOMI OSAKA

When Naomi walked into the heavy storm of cheers and excitement that formed a canopy on the Arthur Ashe Stadium in New York, her heart skipped. She knew at once that the cheers were not for her. Standing on the sun-baked court and watching tons of unfriendly eyes thrusting into her with the precision of a sniper made her tighten her grip on her racket.

The day was Saturday, September 8, 2018. The US Open Finals. It was a much-anticipated showdown between the 36-year-old American 23 Grand Slam winner, Serena Williams, who was out to claim her 24th title, and the 20-year

Japanese, Naomi Osaka, who has yet to pocket a Grand Slam Title in her short career.

The coin was tossed, and Naomi won the right to the very first serve. Naomi knew she needed to put her best foot forward with the first serve. Every second must count. A close look at Naomi's face as she tossed the tennis ball into the air, her arm arched for a perfect hit and feet firmly planted on the court, one would see a sheen of passion and tenacity blazing in her eyes.

As she sent the ball to flight, its force was like a thunderbolt speeding through the night's cloud, precise and loud. It was a warning to the previously excited fans that Naomi wasn't out for a chitchat.

As the match ticked in minutes, Naomi's low-ground penetrating shots, which gave a hard time to Serena, were driven with the precision of an expert archer thrusting seamlessly into the heart of its target.

Serena, with the expert confidence of a martial artist who had won many bouts and knew where exactly to leave a punch that would sink, was strong and fierce like a lion defending her territory. However, Naomi has come up with the perfect antidote for all her monstrous drives.

By the second set, the score was 6-2, 5-4 in Naomi's favor. The two consecutive wins were like bitter pills that ruptured the faces of Serena's fans into a frown. With the match slipping through their fingers, they began sending canon shots of boos to Naomi to prick open her confidence.

With a lead, Naomi built a wall around her confidence, refusing to grant them entry. She continued pushing her way through the match. Naomi's last serve in the final set broke into pointed shards of monstrous swings from both sides of the court.

The crowds, watching the speed with which the ball sped to and fro the court as though it was on some automation, were pulled to the edge of their seats. Finally, Naomi hit a perfect low ground penetrating forehand down the line. Serena was just in time to respond, but it quickly grazed the baseline, scampering out of her reach.

"Game, set, match!" the umpire called. Naomi had won. The final score was 6-2, 6-4. Naomi fell to her knees, crumbled by an iron club of emotion. She had done it. She had won her title. She had defeated her idol. Serena walked over, hugged Naomi, and said, "You played amazing." Naomi, with tears in her eyes, replied, "Thank you so much."

Naomi's win fulfilled a passion that took root in her dad, Leonard. Watching the Williams sisters compete at the 1999 French Open inspired him to introduce his two daughters to tennis. The flame of this inspiration quickly became a wildfire that gulped Naomi's heart.

Naomi Osaka was born on October 16, 1997, in Chūō-ku Osaka, Japan, near the serene waters of Osaka Bay. Born to a Haitian dad, Leonard François, and a Japanese mom, Tamaki Osaka, Naomi grew up under a multicultural family's lively and supportive roof.

At the age of 4, Naomi's dad knew that Japan was not a good soil to plant his daughters' dreams. He loved tennis so much that he moved the whole family from Osaka, Japan, to Long Island, New York, traveling over 6,900 miles.

Growing up in a new environment wasn't going to be a walk in the park for Naomi. It came with challenges. First, she and her sister had to deal with discriminatory comments due to their mixed heritage. Second, being a low-income family, affording adequate tennis training equipment and tournament travel was a strain on the family's budget.

Despite these challenges, her resilience, determination, and the support of her parents, who were her biggest fans, were scaffolds she stepped on to climb over her obstacles and pursue her tennis dreams.

Naomi grew up with a bag of dreams and a head filled with fantasies. Having caught the flu of her father's passion for tennis, she watched many stars like Serena Williams and always imagined herself playing in the Grand Slams. However, success is not a mere fantasy. Passion and dreams were not enough; as her father Leonard often said, "Dreams don't work unless you do".

So, at that young age, with no proper training facilities, Naomi spent countless hours practicing daily. Hitting tennis balls against their garage door. Her hard work and relentless practice paid off, as they helped her breed powerful weapons in her tennis arsenal, which are low ground, fast penetrating serves, and acute quick reflexes, which are weapons she used to break into the spotlight of the tennis world.

The sunny sky of Florida opened its arms wide to Naomi in 2006. This followed her parents' huge decision to relocate to the famous home of sporting activities in the U.S. With its excellent tennis facilities and training programs, Naomi and her sister had access to better opportunities to develop their tennis skills. This set in motion Naomi's break into the tennis world.

December of that same year found Naomi in her first local tennis tournament. The eyes of the crowds who gathered at Harold Avenue Park in Fort Lauderdale, Florida, couldn't miss her powerful baseline shots and swift movement across the court as convincingly won her slightly older opponent. It was this debut that made a mountain of her confidence, planting a firm faith in her ability to achieve anything.

In 2011, at the age of 14, she began training under a coach, Patrick Tauma. Patrick quickly noticed her unique talent and the hunger that burned in her. He tended to her with the patience of a gardener and the encouraging words of a father. He often reminded Naomi, "Your strength lies in your spirit." This made her realize the incredible power of her mind to achieve anything she wanted to.

July 17, 2014, welcomed Naomi to the rough edges of the sports world. It was during her first match in the ITF Women's Circuit. Sixteen-year-old Naomi walked into Amelia Island, Florida, standing on the rooftop of her confidence. The game began with Naomi's more seasoned and composed opponent, Evgeniya Rodina, expertly snuffing out the vast fires of her shots and, in return, dished a mouthful for Naomi.

Naomi, who was not used to such pressure, was overwhelmed. Her emotions swung between anxiety and helplessness. With a racing heart, Naomi desperately struggled to find her rhythm, hunting for the ball. However, her more experienced opponent knew exactly the tender spot to push in the syringe. Naomi chased after the ball like a drowning man trying to hold onto anything. Her opponent exploited it and won the match convincingly.

Naomi broke down in tears after the match. Having watched the game, Coach Patrick knew his next assignment. He needed to teach Naomi that getting her emotions in the way is the easiest way to lose a game, and she must know that it is okay to lose games.

In his words, "Naomi, every champion starts with a loss. What matters is how you rise after you fall. Today was just the beginning of your journey. Keep your head high and keep fighting." These words taught her that the road to greatness is calibrated by the twists and turns of setbacks and the importance of mental toughness.

In 2018, 20-year-old Naomi Osaka stepped onto the court at the BNP Paribas Open to face Daria Kasatkina in the final. The match was a grueling test of endurance, with both players exhausted and tied almost two hours into the game. Despite the pain and fatigue, Naomi refused to give up. In the end, she delivered a powerful shot that clinched the match with a 6-3, 6-2 victory. This win secured her first major title and announced her arrival on the world stage, showcasing the power of passion, resilience, and a strong mindset.

Naomi knew she had no time. With the U.S. Open a month away, she didn't let the euphoria of her victory take her eyes off her goal. She got to work. However, her aspirations for the tournament hit the rocks during a practice session. She sustained a debilitating foot injury that broke her chances.

This hit Naomi, but at this time of her career, she was no stranger to adversity. So, she poured all her energy into her recovery, fighting her way back to the court with the same determination that had propelled her to victory at Indian Wells.

With the support of her coach, Sascha Bajin, who stood by her side, and her iron will, she quickly found her feet to claim her third Grand Slam on September 12, 2020. She defeated Victoria Azarenka in a thrilling three-set match, 1-6, 6-3, 6-3.

This win was particularly significant as Osaka used the tournament to raise awareness about social justice issues, wearing masks with the names of Black victims of violence. Her victory, both on and off the court, cemented her status as a powerful athlete and advocate.

Even with her impressive wins, Naomi, like every other athlete, was not yet immune to losses. However, the 2021 U.S. Open loss to much younger Canadian opponent Leylah Fernandez hit her hard. She was defeated in the third round of a match that ended with a score of 5-7, 7-6(2), 6-4. After the loss, Osaka opened up on her struggles with mental health, announcing a break from tennis to focus on her well-being.

But Naomi's story of resilience didn't end there. She made her comeback in 2022, showing her determination by reaching the Miami Open final and continuing to inspire others with her commitment to both her sport and her personal growth.

Naomi's career trajectory is inspiring despite facing challenges such as poor background, injuries, and mental health issues. Her confidence in her abilities was the powerhouse that fueled her determination to win. Hence, at the center of her incredible achievements were the words, "You have to believe in yourself when no one else does,"

Speak your Mind

Have you ever had days when you feel tired or upset, even when doing something you usually love, like playing sports or spending time with friends? Have you ever felt anxious about going to practice a sport you have so much or doing something you love doing?

What did you do when you felt this way? Did you go ahead to play in the sports, or did you talk to your parents or coach?

Your Well-being Comes First

It is important to speak up when you're having mental struggles, even if it's something you usually love doing. Naomi Osaka, one of the best tennis players in the world, faced challenges with her mental health, even though she loved tennis.

Sometimes, you might feel sad, anxious, or overwhelmed when doing activities you enjoy, like sports, art, or schoolwork. These feelings might mean you need to talk to someone. It's okay to tell a parent, teacher, or coach how you feel. Just like Naomi took a break from tennis to take care of herself, it is essential to take breaks and ask for help when needed. Remember, your well-being comes first.

DIANA TAURASI

This night was unusual. Even Diana Taurasi's favorite Nike shoe could tell with how her feet rattled inside it. The weight of expectations of the 7,564 spectators gathered at Footprint Center arena in Phoenix, Arizona, to witness history in the making weighed on her.

Diana was just 18 points shy from becoming the first woman in the history of the NBA to hit 10,000 career points. With each tick of the clock ripening, the hope on the expectant faces of her fans and her mother was visible.

As she watched the crowd before the starting whistle, she thought of 2017, when in her hometown of Los Angeles, before a home crowd and in the presence of her childhood idol, Bryant Kobe, she broke Tina Thompson's all-time scoring record of 7,488[th] career points to take the top spot on WNBA's all-time scoring list.

Diana was not just out to break a record on August 3, 2023, but ready to set one.

The game started, and after the first and second quarters, Diana only managed to make five points in each quarter. It seems that the weight of expectations had robbed her of her agility, leading to a slow start. But as always, excuse is an effective weapon she had never learned to use.

In the third quarter of the game that night, her favorite mantra, "I am not afraid of anyone…" found its way into her mind. It fired up every pulse that held the balance of her 41-year-old nerves. It fired up her quick-footed deep purple Lebron 17 2k edition shoes that began to glide with swift seamlessness around the court.

But before the night of August 3, 2023, took a pen to write Diana perpetually into history, her parents, Mario and Lilliana Taurasi, Argentine immigrants, began the "once upon a time" that launched us into the world of Diana story by deciding to immigrate into the US in 1978 to Chino in California.

On 11th June 1982, in Glendale, California, Mario Taurasi, a former professional Italian soccer player, and Liliana, whose heart burnt with the passionate Argentine warmth, made history by birthing Diana Taurasi.

Diana grew up in Chino in a close-knit family steeped in Spanish roots, with her sister Jessica, who was two years older than her, her father a renowned goalie of Italian soccer, and her ever-supportive mother with a large heart.

In an interview many years later, she mentioned her family's tremendous impact on her. In her words: "I kind of grew up in a different kind of family atmosphere, and that's what made me. It was always dinner at eight every night. Our family, our unit. And that's how I treat my team. It's our unit. Our family. And that's what has carried me through all these years in the WNBA, oversees, Olympic teams, UConn_all teams are my family".

In her suburban home with an athletic father, it was not surprising that Diana and her sister were interested in sports. Diana loved soccer, a trait she inherited from her goalie father. In the same athletic spirit, she loved Basketball.

Just before she turned fifteen, the WNBA had not come into existence, so her interest in the game was nurtured by her father and the Lakers, who were her favorite. In Chino, while attending Don Hugo High School with her sister, she began building her muscles for what would be an illustrious career.

Watching her young feet and budding arms throbbing with passion in Don Hugo's high school court, it was unsurprising that in 1996, in her first international tournament and overseas trip, the fourteen-year-old Diana was drafted into the USA squad that went to Ma del Plalaa, Argentina.

In 2000, after an illustrious display of talent, skill, and excellence, 18-year-old Diana was jointly named the national high school player of the year by Naismith and Parade magazine.

At this point, Diana was already in love with Basketball. Her conflict of interest between soccer and basketball had evaporated. Now, she left herself to be possessed by the game and lived out one invaluable lesson that sits in the heart of her career: to chase excellence rather than success.

She would clearly express this later, when years of hard work and excellence had landed her pretty in the hall of fame, when she said, "I never for once want to be or talked about or worked every single day to be the best player in the world. I just try to be the best basketball player that day."

It was this mindset that took her to the University of Connecticut, where her above-average basketball IQ didn't go unnoticed. She was drafted into the UConn team.

While at UConn, she was a queen who ruled in court with her dexterous, stone-cold killer prowess. She played as a point guard and shooting guard, inspiring her teammates and changing the game for everyone.

During her time in Storrs, UConn basked in the glory of an overall mark of 139-8. She became the first player in its history to total 2,000 points, 6000 assists, and 600 rebounds in a career. She guided them to their three consecutive national championships and became the first two-time national player of the year.

It was on the wings of these achievements that she became the number one overall draft pick in the 2004 WNBA Draft by the Phoenix Mercury. It was here that she was officially launched into the world of the Women's National Basketball League.

In Mercury, Diana came with her magic wand: her talent, passion, clinical skills, and discipline. The very engine that has powered her into early stardom. A crest that kept her sturdy, denying age a taste of her youthful vitality.

Before Diana came to Mercury in 2004, they struggled in the league. But Diana came and was simply incredible. She led the team with an average of 17 points and 3.9 assists per game, dragging them from a worst-season record of 8-26 in 2003 to a 17-17 finish in 2004.

This impressive debut season led to her being named the Rookie of the Year and launching her into the first of her 10-first Team All WNBA honors that season.

Diana was so incredibly good that her then Coach in UConn, Geno Aurelima, had so much faith in her abilities that he would always declare to his opponents, "We have Diana, and you don't!".

Her love, obsession, passion, and skill for basketball birthed the Thursday night of August 3, 2023, where this story began. Diana became a live wire early in the third quarter after a glance at the screen near the right wing outside the 3-point line. The screen showed she was seated at 9,997 points. She needed only just three points for her big break.

A hunger enveloped her. The hunger was so palpable that even when the Atlanta Dreams double team cordoned off her, they were not enough stomach to contain the hunger rumbles in her heart. She was just looking for one thing: the chance to get a shoot.

Then, it came. In swift seconds, her 41-year-old skillful body wriggled free from the double-team cordon of Atlanta's defense to make her hungrily outstretched arms home for a deep pass from Moriah Jefferson, 28 feet away from the basket. The time was 8.23 minutes in the third quarter when her masterful arm seamlessly gave birth to history with a 3-pointer.

Boom! voices erupted in hearty cheers: hugging, shouting, and giving room for drops of joyous tears to have a field day. She has done it. This was the climax of the night. Diana, in the euphoria of one who has lived up to a promise, took a jubilant walk down to her side of the court with arms spread wide, bringing her teammates into an embrace that said, "You made this happen."

She did not forget her fans, her parents, and everyone who came to see her make history again. So, after the game, which would later end in a 91-71 win over the Atlanta Dream, with Diana finishing with 42 points (the highest she had made in a game since 2010 and has scored in regulation in her career), she made her way around the court, signing autographs, and going into the stands to greet fans.

Diana's reaching out to her teammates and fans to celebrate, something she rarely did, announced the heart of gratitude of one who understands that success is teamwork and that others play significant roles in our success.

At age 41, that night's game would make her the oldest player with a 40-point game in WNBA history.

However, Diana's journey wasn't all rosy. On May 16, 2021, at age 38, in a match against the Sun, where she finished with 19 points in 29 minutes of action, she suffered a chest injury. She had a sternum fracture (a fracture of the flat bone in the center of the chest). The fracture made her miss about four weeks of play.

Here is the surprising and inspiring thing about this injury: It didn't take away Diana's fighting spirit. Even before a CT scan revealed the fracture, she went on to play two subsequent games against the Mystic and Connecticut, scoring 17 and 13 points, respectively. It was after this that she took a break to heal. Although her hands were off the game in those moments, her heart was in it.

On June 27, 2021, in her first game, after missing the court of play for a month due to a fractured sternum, she came back in style, scoring 25 points against Los Angeles to reach her 9000th career point. This is a testament that our challenges shouldn't deter us but strengthen us.

Apart from Diana reaching her 10,000th career point milestone, she had a backlog of achievements. She was the WNBA league's all-time leading scorer in 2017. Between 2001 and 2004, she made a name for herself as a member of the US Women's basketball teams that won five consecutive Olympic gold medals.

She is one of the only twelve players in WNBA history to have earned a world championship gold medal, an Olympic gold medal, an NCAA title, and a WNBA championship.

Diana is the second most decorated FIBA athlete on the planet, with five Olympic gold medals and three FIBA World Cup bronze medals over a two-decade basketball career. She was a four-time USA female athlete of the year from 2006, 2010, 2012 to 2016, 2010, and 2018 All FIBA World Cup teams; 2008 FIBA Diamond Ball All-Tournament team; 3-point trophy winner at the 2006 World Cup; and 2001 FIBA All Junior World Cup (U-19).

Undisputably, the hallmark of Diana Taurasi's illustrious career is love, passion, hard work, and teamwork. It is on the wings of these that she had soared. This is why, even at age 42, she's not showing any weakness in her wings but has continued flying higher into the limelight.

Speak your Mind

Can you think of a time when you had to keep going even though you were physically or emotionally tired, like during a tough practice or a challenging day at school?

How did you handle it, and what did you learn from that experience?"

Persevering Through Injury

Taurasi has battled multiple injuries throughout her career, yet she continues to perform at a high level, often playing through pain to lead her team to victory.

Mental toughness involves pushing through physical and emotional pain, knowing that perseverance is vital to long-term success.

FLOYD MAYWEATHER

The cliché of making lemonades with bitter lemons life throws at you did not make much sense until Friday in the Atlanta Olympics, 1996. The eager crowd at the Alexander Memorial Coliseum indoor arena had come to watch the rising American amateur boxing sensation, 19-year-old Floyd Mayweather Jr.

This would be his first-ever international debut in the featherweight (57 Kilogram. An equivalent of 125 pound) boxing category. Mayweather Jr, with a rare combination of his incredible fast footwork, patient counter punches, instinctive defensive techniques, speed, and power, which wears his opponents out, offering him the room to gift them a definite punch.

However, trouble set in paradise in his semifinal match against the 27-year-old two-time Olympian Serafim Todorov of Bulgaria. A match from which he would eventually make lemonades that would fuel his passion and success throughout his boxing career.

Seconds into round one of the match, the punches of the visibly threatened Todorov were all over the place. Still, they couldn't penetrate the vigorous defense of Mayweather, whose accurate punches easily slipped into Todorov to make an impact. Yet sadly, before anyone could say Jack, the scoreboard read 2-0 in favor of Todorov, who was yet to land a definitive punch.

Before continuing the story, Let's talk about how Mayweather Jr. spent his whole life defending himself, turning the bricks life threw into a strong power punch that landed him fame.

Born on the 24th of February 1977 into a troublesome neighborhood and a poor, chaotic family in Grand Rapids, Michigan, to a father who was a drug dealer and a mother who was a drug addict, one can imagine how chaotic the early life of Floyd Joyce Sinclair was. Mayweather Jnr was named after his mother at birth.

This was the very first challenge Floyd Sinclair faced as a child. So, even before he knew how to fold his palms into fists and throw punches, his environment already gave him a rule: to survive, you must fight your way through.

This rule explains his incredible defensive skills in the ring, which earned him the nickname "pretty boy" among his amateur comrades. This was because his impressive defensive skill was so good that it never gave anyone a chance to punch his face, thereby leaving it with no address of punches.

Growing up in Rapids, Floyd Sinclair's father, Mayweather Sr., was everything a father should not be. He nevertheless tried to be present for his children. He never lost consciousness of his environment and the need to groom his son to adapt and survive. Being a successful professional boxer, he introduced Floyd Sinclair into the family tradition as soon as he could walk.

Floyd Sinclair's dad always took him to the gym and held him up to hit speed bags. It was from here that his love for boxing was born. As a kid wandering the streets of Rapids, he was known as the boy who threw air punches. He was so obsessed with the sport that at only age 7, he got fitted with his first pair of boxing gloves. His speed and incredibly unique style made waves at the local gym and filtered into every household in Rapids. Soon, he became a sensation.

To appropriately wear his newly found fame, Floyd Sinclair immersed himself in the Mayweather boxing tradition. A tradition of which his professional boxing uncles, Jeff Mayweather and Roger Mayweather, were part. With this, he dropped his birthname, Sinclair, and took up his father's name, Mayweather. And so he became Floyd Mayweather Jnr: a name on whose shoulder he would ride throughout his career.

As early as age 9, things began to go south for Mayweather Jr. He was sent to the Hiram Square neighborhood, Brunswick, New Jersey, to stay with his mom, Deborah, who was a drug addict, and her relatives with whom he would have to cramp in a one-bedroom apartment.

Staying with his mom and watching her shrink by substance abuse had a significant toll on him as he lacked the care he should have gotten. With a chaotic home that continuously threatened to rob him of his sanity, he made the local gym his new home, spending all his time there. It was his escape.

He continued this way with only a bag of hope, determination, and courage until 1993, when his dedication pulled out a silver lining. It was here, in 1993, when he was just 16, that he had his first official fight. It was his amateur debut. After the debut, he earned his first national Golden Gloves.

Just when Mayweather Jr. thought his dream had come alive, his father, who was then his coach and trainer, was arrested for illegal drug trafficking and sentenced to five years in jail. This shattered Mayweather Jr. Being an amateur boxer, this was enough to break him. But instead of being broken, he took up the responsibility of fending for himself.

Things got so bad that he told his grandmother, Bernice Mayweather, who was solely covering up for the absence of his parents, that he wanted to get a job to help with the house finances. The grandmother saw the potential he had. In Mayweather Jr.'s words, "I think my grandmother saw my potential first," he said. It is because of this potential that his grandmother saw that made her respond to Mayweather Jr's request with "No, just keep boxing.".

This was the fire that kept Mayweather Jr. burning. The young Mayweather, confident that all he wanted to do was boxing, later dropped out of Ottawa High School to give his whole being to boxing. Although his decision might seem rash, it showed a particular attribute of Mayweather: his stunning decisiveness in the ring and the accuracy of his punches.

His zeal and passion for his craft shone brightly in 1994 and 1996, when he won the national Golden Gloves again, making it a treble in his amateur career. His impressive record of just six losses in 84 matches in his amateur career fetched him a spot in the Atlanta Olympics.

Now, back to the Olympics story we started earlier, we can easily see going by the rollercoaster of personal history, which the young Mayweather had to surmount to be at the Olympics, he didn't cower even in the face of the drama that took place at Alexander Memorial Coliseum indoor arena.

In the second round of the fight, Mayweather quickly leveled up, bringing the score to 7-6, with definite punches that jerked back Todorov's head, causing an instinctive yelp among the spectators. After that, Mayweather threw two combinations and decisively drove four punches into Todorove's face while

Todorov resorted merely to slapping Mayweather with the strap of his gloves. Surprisingly, no points were given to Mayweather. After the fighters went down, Todrov was magically ahead by 8-7.

However, with the result of the match yet to be announced, the spectators who had watched the 19-year-old Mayweather decisively pummel Todorov in the ring knew that Mayweather already had the day. The match referee, Hamadi Shouman, who watched the two fighters sweat it out from a close quarter, did not doubt that Mayweather had won.

When the announcer's voice rang out, "And the winner is…" the referee was already in the characteristic format of declaring a winner in each bout raised Mayweather's hand. But then the surprise that shook everyone came when the announcer called out, "Serafim Todorov of Bulgaria."

The visibly shocked match referee craned his neck to see the overhead scoreboard. Disbelief sat on his face when he saw a 10-9 score in favor of Todorov. The faces of the once jubilant U.S fans crumpled into an orchestra of revolting boos at the decision.

Sadly, even the protest filed by the US team leader Gerald Smith couldn't save the day. This led to the untimely resignation of Bill Waeckerie, one of the international judges, immediately after the bout.

In his words, "the judging was totally incompetent' and "the system is not capable of correcting itself with the people currently in charge of selecting and assigning officials."

Mayweather reaction to this daylight robbery was surprising. After the match, he said, "I got ripped off. But that's the boxing game, you have to live with it." Although he was pained, he went ahead and fought for third place, settling for the bronze medal. In an interview after the tournament, he'd say, "I know I won. I'm proud of what I did. I represented my country. When I go home, I want everyone to be as happy as if it was a goal medal".

Two lessons stand out here: the ability to give our best at every point so that even when things don't go our way, we will know in our hearts that we did our best, and the importance of never quitting because things didn't go our way.

Later on in 2020, twenty years after the Olympic loss, in an interview with Football legend Shannon Sharpe, when asked about how he felt about the loss, he said, "It made me work that much harder as a professional not to feel that pain again." When probed further by Shape, he insisted, "That was the best thing that happened to me-one of the best things."

True to his word, that match would be the last match Mayweather lost in his amateur career before his mind-boggling illustrious professional career, where after over twenty years, he never lost a game. He earned fifteen major world championships and had a perfect career record of 50-0.

He won twenty-seven of his fights, more than half of the fights in his career by knockouts. Immediately after the Olympics, he launched himself into professional boxing. The Olympic loss taught him one lesson evident in his professional career: to be decisive with his finishing off opponents in each bout to leave no room for any doubt about the winner.

This played out firstly in his debut professional bout with Apodoca (for whom the match was also his professional debut) on October 11, 1996, at Texas Station Casino, Las Vegas, Nevada, just two months after the Olympics.

In the first round, Mayweather connected a hook that crumbled Apodaca to one knee. Mayweather had successfully driven into Apodaco 30 out of the 60 punches he threw in the first round, while Apodaca, with luck, only managed to slip in 2 out of his 30 punches.

The match ref, Kenny Bayless, had to end the match when the now helpless Apodaca, was knocked down again by Mayweather's left hook just thirty seconds into the second round.

Since then, Mayweather Jr. never looked back. He continued his streak, climbing through the ranks from light Welterweight to Light Welterweight, welterweight, and Light Middleweight, returning to welterweight and fighting big names in the boxing world.

When Mayweather was at the peak of his career, it seemed the shadow of his troublesome and chaotic family background had a firm grip on him. He had a fiery temper and a habit of trash-talking inside and outside the ring. This played out in the litany of legal issues he had that could easily be avoided if he had it together.

Of particular significance was the issue of domestic violence. This burnt cold the love some of his fans had for him. On May 12, 2012, he began serving terms for domestic battery of his high school sweetheart and partner, Josie Harris, who was also the mother of his three kids. After about sixty days of incarceration, he was released, and he once again devoted himself to his craft.

However, despite his numerous shortcomings, no one can deny that Mayweather was meant for boxing. His relentless hard work, towering self-confidence, fierceness, speed, unrivaled unique defensive skills, and flexibility to quickly adapt to his opponents' unique styles made a boulevard for his illustrious career as one of the best to ever grace the rings until his retirement on August 26, 2017.

Floyd Mayweather loved his gloves so much that even a chaotic family and unfair treatment in the 1996 Atlanta Olympics could not stop him. He used his cheered gloves to punch himself into the limelight.

Speak your Mind

Can you think of a time when you tried hard at something, like a school project, sports game, or art competition, but things didn't turn out how you hoped?

What is that one thing you did after facing the disappointment? What did you learn from that experience?

Have you ever been disappointed when someone you looked up to let you down? For example, a coach not picking you for the team, a teacher not recognizing your hard work, or a friend breaking a promise?

How did it make you feel, and what did you learn?

Handling Disappointment

Floyd Mayweather is a perfect example of how to handle disappointment. Early in his career, he faced challenges and setbacks, including controversial decisions that didn't go his way. Instead of letting these disappointments break him, Mayweather used them as motivation to improve.

He focused on refining his skills, training harder, and staying mentally tough. His undefeated record in professional boxing shows how handling disappointment with determination can lead to greatness. The lesson here is to turn setbacks into stepping stones, using disappointment as fuel to achieve your goals.

SIMEONE BILES

Watching the tumbling and flipping of the teen girls who practiced in the gym, the only thing that came into the mind of six-year-old Simeone was, "I think I can do this." And just like that, her heart caught the fire of passion. Without waiting for approval, instinctively, she began her flips, copying the girls she had seen.

While her daycare classmates were on the field trip with her, engaged in sightseeing at the gym, Simeone had already foreseen her future, found her dream, and began living it.

"Have you done this before?" a voice asked. It was the voice of Aimee Boorman, who became the young Simone's coach for most of her career. After watching Simone perform her flips with effortless rhythm, she instantly knew she had found a star. Commenting on Simone's genius and physicality years later in an interview, Boorman said. "That was just kinetic energy from her body. I was like, 'Wow, this kid is something".

After that encounter with Simone at the gym, Aimee Boorman sent a note to Simone's home, marking the beginning of Simone's journey to greatness. This was how the story of the girl, whose air maneuvers and delicate twists and turns in the air, would grow to become the most decorated gymnast in history. Before we talk about the content of that note, let's go back to the starting point of Simone's life journey.

Born in Columbus, Ohio, on the 14th of March 1997 to parents who were drug and alcohol addicts, her father abandoned her and her three siblings to their mom, Shannon, at a young age.

At the age of two, Simone and her siblings were taken to a foster home because their mother was both unfit and incapable of taking care of them. However, luck came running to them when Ronn Biles, their mother's father, and his sister decided to adopt them. Simone, who was three, and her younger sister Adria were adopted by Ronn Biles and Nellie, his wife, while Simone's elder brother stayed with their maternal aunt.

Growing up in Spring, Texas, a suburb of Houston, under the effective care of Ronn Biles, an Air Force Veteran, and Nellie, a trained nurse who ran a string of nursing homes in Houston, Simone had a secure and supportive environment that made room for her abundant energy to be harnessed and channeled into a passion that set aflame the world of gymnastics.

This journey began with that note that came into the home of the Biles, urging them to enroll the young Simone into a regular gymnastics class. The Biles didn't sleep on this, having already noticed that Simone had enough energy to last her a lifetime. They enrolled her in a training program at Bannon Gymnastics in Houston under the exceptional tutelage of Coach Aimee Boorman.

Once she started training at Bannon, she quickly mastered complex routines, from perfecting her balance beam technique to executing flawless floor exercise flips. She seamlessly slipped into the demanding regimen that would have easily tired out other kids her age, soon becoming a star in the gym.

However, Simone's energetic personality was a shadow that held onto her like a leech. It followed her wherever she went, even to school. The keen eyes of her teachers couldn't help but notice how Simone easily gets distracted and unable to sit still while in class. A diagnosis revealed that at the root of her restless energy was ADHD: Attention Deficit Hyperactivity Disorder.

Although a Ritalin stimulant (a drug that can help increase the ability to pay attention) was prescribed for her, her foster mother, Nellie, with her years of experience, knew that Ritalin wouldn't carry all the workload of keeping focused. So, she stepped in with a routine of helping Simone draw up a daily to-do list and, in later years, a list of goals that she divided into short-term and long-term, which she planned to achieve that year.

This became the strong foundation that skyrocketed Simone's successful career. With Simone's energy properly channeled, her work rate improved tremendously both at the gym and in school.

The clouds began to gather in 2011. It was going to rain. It would be the first official rain that would launch the reign of an illustrious career. It was Simone's first official appearance in public performance. She was just 14, freshly out from the comfort of Bannon Gymnastics, where she was a star. Now, she would compete with other stars at the American Classic in Houston for the junior national competition for a spot in the junior national team.

Simone arrived at the competition with a bag full of hopes. As soon as the competition began, she discovered it wasn't a walk in the park. Here, she suffered her first heartbreak in the demanding sport of gymnastics. She finished 14th in the competition, missing the 13-man national team list by a spot.

This defeat would create a hole in her heart. A hole constantly filled with self-doubt in her mind, and later anxiety and imposter syndrome that would haunt her throughout her career. In her Memoir Courage to Soar, she wrote about how she felt about the incident, "That's how my journey as an elite gymnast began _ with a defeat that put an ache in my heart and doubts in my mind."

Though a sad tale, there is a sweet lesson we can learn from it: that it is okay to get angry and cry when, despite our best efforts, we don't achieve a set goal at a set time. But we must also learn to gather ourselves, pocket our fears, and try again (harder this time). This was exactly what Simone did.

After her defeat, she dedicated herself entirely to her passion. She switched to homeschooling, giving up public school to pour all her time and effort into gymnastics.

Simone's move proves that success is a costly undertaking. Her sacrifice began to bear enormous fruits in 2012. It started with returning to the same competition that first took her smiles: the American Classic. This time, she finished first place in the vault and all-around competition, tied for second in the floor exercises, and placed third in the floor exercises. With this, she was named to the junior national team, achieving her first milestone.

Given her impressive performance at the 2012 Classic, Simone became a name that sits on the lips of every gymnastics lover. She was the favorite for the 2012 Olympics but was a few months below the age requirement. Her new fame was a good thing for her. Slowly, this awareness began to climb over her, and she realized the weight of expectations that came with it. This led to one of the worst performances in her career that would once again bruise her confidence.

It was in 2013, at the US Secret Classic. All eyes were on the young rising star, Simone. She could feel the weight of expectations in the excited eyes of the spectators weighing on her. With a strong desire to live up to expectations, she lost her composure and couldn't focus. It began with her continuous missteps on the balance beam until she completely lost control and fell face down.

The floor exercises weren't any better. She couldn't get her nerves together, and she fell several times. Boorman, her visibly scared coach, had to pull her out of the meet for her safety, abruptly ending her participation. This was another heartbreak.

The incident significantly watered down her self-confidence. It was so bad that she had to see a sports psychologist for two weeks, even against her wish. However, that experience, coupled with the support of friends and family,

Simone said, "That helped me get in tune with myself so that I felt more comfortable with myself and less anxious"

With this, she learned to channel her energy on enjoying the sport rather than performing solely for the benefit of others. This would inform her usual quote, "I'm not the next Usain Bolt or Michael Phelps. I'm the Simone Biles".

Twenty-one days later, after the disastrous outing, she was officially named to the Senior National Team after she won the USA Gymnastics National Championship.

This was followed by her first international title at the World Gymnastic Championship Antwerp, Belgium, where she took home two gold medals and the coveted all-around title, making her the first black woman to win gold in all-around events.

In Antwerp, Simone came with her superpowers. She didn't give room to her fears. Here, she introduced one of the most complex and jaw-breaking movements on the floor exercises into the history of gymnastics. It would be named after her. It was called the Biles. The Biles is a double layout with a half twist. Here, the gymnast does a double flip with the legs straightened, throwing a half twist at the end. This means that the gymnast would land facing the very direction she was running from.

With these achievements, she stamped her feet firmly in the world of gymnastics. Between 2014 and 2015, at just 17 of age, she pocketed four World championship golds. She would crown it with her first Olympics: Rio 2016. Here, her superpower was a blinking light. She made a clean sweep of gold in the all-around, team, vault, and floor exercises and then bronze on the balance beam.

With her success in the Olympics and the World Championship competition, she bagged nineteen medals, making her the most decorated American gymnast of all time. After the tournament, with the ovation still very high and the thirteen years of her active career playing before her fulfilled eyes, she knew she needed some break. And she took it.

By the time Simone returned to public competitions in 2018, after her 711 days off, the most challenging moments of her career were just around the corner, waiting for her: the Tokyo Olympics. The general expectation of her enthusiastic fans was that she would cement her dominance in gymnastics in that tournament.

The Olympics kicked off in July 2021. While the teams prepared, a battle raged in Simone's mind. Her mental health has come under fire. A few days into the tournament, with the hope of her fans rising, she made headlines with the news that shocked everyone. She was withdrawing from the Olympic tournament.

Simone had developed twisties. This is a dangerous situation for a gymnast, as it causes them to lose control of themselves and feel lost in the air while performing their twists and turns in air movement. This raised lots of pressure, criticism, and disappointment among her fans. Simone didn't want to risk an injury and her teammates' efforts. She didn't bow to the pressure; instead, she took time off to get herself in shape.

Withdrawing meant she wouldn't defend her Olympic titles, but she clung to her courage and walked. Simone's decision comes with an important message: our health should always come first in our careers.

Simone, fully rejuvenated, made a unique comeback to the gymnastic scene on August 2023 to clinch her eighth U.S. all-around title after her impressive performance at the US classic. With that, she had set a record as the oldest American gymnast to secure all-around titles. Then, in October 2023, she took home her 21st World Championship gold medal at the World Artistic Gymnastics Championship in Antwerp, Belgium, thereby winning her 6th all-around title.

But Simone is not done yet. At 27, for one whose sports involve a lot of wear and tear that could easily cut one off, Simone, after overwhelmingly winning the U.S. Olympic Team Trials for gymnastics, is warming up for her third Olympics appearance in Paris in 2024.

Speak your Mind

Can you think of a time when you gave up some playtime, screen time, or a fun outing with friends to finish your homework, help with chores, learn some skills, or practice a sport?

How did it feel then? What did you achieve because of that choice? Are you happy to do it again in the future? Can you think of something else you can sacrifice now for something bigger in the future?

Sacrificing to Achieve More.

Simone Biles is a powerful example of sacrificing to achieve more. From a young age, she devoted countless hours to training, often missing out on typical childhood activities. She even made the tough decision to move away from home to be closer to her coach.

These sacrifices allowed her to focus intensely on her goals, leading her to become one of the most decorated gymnasts in history. Simone's story shows that to reach the highest levels of success, you sometimes have to give up small, immediate pleasures for the sake of a bigger dream.

NOVAK DJOKOVIC

Anxiety built a bridge between the two famous archrivals in tennis history. They faced each other like predators who knew and acknowledged each other's peculiar strengths. They were aware that any miscalculation would lead to an unhappy ending.

Even if one were too deaf to hear the echoes of exhausted pulses of the two men who are battling it out on the clay court of Philippe Chatrier, Roland Garros in Paris, one's eye would not miss the restless buttocks of the spectators whom suspense and plot twists created by the fierce combatants pulled to the very edge of their seats.

The year was 2013 and it is the French Open. It was the semifinal match between Novak Djokovic, the World No. 1 in tennis, and Rafael Nadal, the king of Clay Court. If Djokovic defeats Nadal, he would be the second player to have done it since Nadal took control of the clay court in Roland Garros in 2005.

But with their current back and forth in the court: with Nadal leading in the first set by 6-4, Novak closing the second set with a 6-3 win, Nadal finishing up the third set in a 6-1 win, and Novak punishing Nadal for his errors in the fourth set with a 7-6 win, they are now in the fifth set with Novak Djokovic leading 4-3. This would just be the one occasion someone takes Nadal to a fifth set in a semifinal match in Garros.

The sweat that bled through both men, the uneasiness in the swing of their already aching arms, showed they were already spent. But this was war. Djokovic needed to get to the finals to fulfill the dream of his early career coach, Jelena Gencic.

Gencic died a week before the French Open and had wanted him to get the trophy. It was the only trophy he hadn't won in his illustrious career. This was his fifth attempt. He can't let it slip away.

Nadal, on his part, was already beaten the previous year at the 2012 Australian Open. It was a grueling five-hour and fifty-three-minute match that ended in a 7-5 win in favor of Djokovic. It was a payback time for Nadal. Moreover, this was Roland Garros. His clay court. No one beats him in his kingdom.

True to his word, with a better mastery in the clay court, Nadal pounced on the defining moment in the fifth set when Djokovic presented it: in the split seconds that came on the heels of Djokovic losing his balance in a desperate smash and crashing into the net. This was followed by netting a forehand, leveling the game to 4-4. Nadal. Like the master he was, he took the chance. In the 45th minute, he took hold of the driver's seat in the game and drove to victory in a 9 to 7 lead.

This was the epic rivalry that would sit in the heart of every tennis lover. As expected, the match visibly shattered Djokovic. He was so close to winning when his fortune was turned. He had desperately needed that win. Speaking to Kate Battersby after the match, he said, "I wanted this title so much, so I am disappointed. It's not the end of the world. The feeling is not great at the moment, but I have years in front of me. I will come back, and I will keep trying to win it", he said.

With this, Djokovic not only showed a rare spirit of sportsmanship but also gave something everyone on a journey to success should have: hope. This has been the spirit of Djokovic throughout his career. He was a man with a bag full of hope. He was a fighter who didn't sulk whenever he lost a game.

Talking about games, let's uncover how the game of life played out for Novak Djokovic from birth.

It all began on May 22, 1987, in Belgrade, Yugoslavia (present Serbia), when Djokovic was born to a ski coach father who was also a pro in football. With an uncle and an aunt who were both professional skiers, growing up in a family with sports in their bloodstream, as expected, sports took a larger space in their hearts. The young Djokovic was set to follow the tradition. But at age four, Djokovic took a different sports path that his two siblings would later follow: Tennis.

It began with his father gifting him a tennis racket and a ball. This would become his favorite toy, which would swing him into fame. With the racket and his parents' sports complex, which housed two restaurants and a lawn tennis court, Djokovic had a perfect breeding ground for his immense talent.

At first, his parents must have thought it was some childhood obsession that would wear off with time. But time, when it came, didn't have enough muscle to loosen Djokovic genius hands from the shaft of the racket. He held on till 1993 when Jelena Gencic, a Yugoslavian tennis legend who would coach him for the next six years, discovered him.

But the war that ravaged Yugoslavia during this time came and sat beside Djokovic dream. The war sucked up Belgrade, Djokovic's hometown, with a bomb. During the battle, Djokovic and his parents spent most of their time in the basement of the family house.

After the war, with his dream of being a professional sportsman still very much alive, his parents subsequently spent a fortune to send him to Pilic Academy in Munich, Germany, at age 13 to pursue a career in tennis. It was here that his immense talent found wings to fly into stardom.

Barely a year into the academy, he gathered enough expertise to begin his international career. It began in 2001 when, in a team competition, he represented Yugoslavia at the World Junior Championship, bagging a silver medal. He was 14, but he had the mind of a genius.

Before the year drew its curtains, he had pocketed triple European champion in singles, doubles, and team competitions. He quickly moved up the ranks in 2003, at age 16, after winning five International Tennis Federation (ITF) tournaments. With this, he placed himself on the global map, ranking 40th best junior tennis player globally.

Djokovic officially turned pro in 2003. Since then, after he won his first Association of Tennis Challenger in 2004 in Budapest, Hungary, he worked his way into the Top 100 in the world after qualifying at Wimbledon in 2005, reaching the third round of the tournament. He has never looked back.

It's been almost two decades since the 17-year-old was named in the Top 100 in the world. And now, with dedication and consistency, he has worked his way to becoming the World's number one. In the long tightrope that separates these years, he has won 24 Grand Slams and, in thirteen different years, pocketed first place in the world of tennis: an incredible feat. But like the DNA of every legend, setbacks held him by the throat.

The one thing that has trailed Djokovic early in his career has been his health. He gained a notorious reputation for always withdrawing midway into a match. He was like a busy train that always carried different ailments. He always retired due to heat exhaustion, dizziness, blurred vision, and cramps, among other things.

Although his exceptional brilliance on the court showed he was a star, his poor physicality set a canopy of doubts that shadowed his ability to last in the sports. Players and fans saw his frequent withdrawal and injury breaks as a tactic he used to distract his opponents.

One such withdrawal that left a permanent dent in his illustrious career took place on Wednesday, June 7, 2006. It was his first quarterfinals with the defending champion Nadal Rafael in the French Open at Roland Garros.

Djokovic didn't start the game on a good foot. He lost his first service games, giving a massive advantage to Nadal, who punished him for that with a decisive lead.

Although Djokovic would try to save the situation by holding Nadal's serve with a nerve-wracking forehand that startled Nadal, it didn't look like a day Nadal would let him win. Before anyone could say Jack, Nadal had already claimed the first set with a 6-4 lead.

Even at this, hope still held up the steady eyebrows of the crowd who waited for magic from Djokovic in the second set. It did not take too long in the second set before the crowd's hope began to tank. It began when Djokovic started to take a medical break due to a lower back injury.

With a known history of withdrawing in games, the crowds believed it was one of his stunts. Although he put up an impressive performance, he still lost to Nadal, 6-4. By the third game of the third set, Djokovic's back had become completely sore, and he retired from the game, giving Nadal a safe entry into the Semifinals.

Another unfortunate incident was in the Quarter Finals of the US Open, 2008. Even before the match, a bad blood already found its way between Djokovic and Andy Roddick. So, in an interview before his encounter with Djokovic, Andy threw shades at Djokovic frequent ailments.

The bitter comments would serve as fuel for Djokovic, who finished off Andy in four quick sets. Although Andy's shades ate into Djokovic and even turned the infuriated crowd against him.

Commenting on the crowd's reaction, he said, "They are already against me because they think I'm faking everything. That was not nice....I have sixteen injuries and I'm faking it. The momentum is not nice."

This was a challenging moment for Djokovic. But then, true to his resilient career spirit, instead of sulking or folding to the weight of the criticisms, he did what anyone wants to be a star does: seeking a solution for his condition.

In his desperate search, he started with nasal surgery. Later, he moved on to yoga, but nothing changed. He changed coaches, workouts, and trainers, but nothing changed. But he didn't give up.

In 2011, he hired a nutritionist from Cyprus. In a dramatic twist of fate, the presence of the nutritionist saved him from what would have been a disastrous career. With the nutritionist, he discovered that the primary cause of his health woes was spaghetti. With this, he was introduced to a gluten-free diet, taking off bread, pasta, and finally, his favorite: pizza from his diet.

The change of diet waved a magic wand on Djokovic career. In his book, "Serve to Win," he said, "Once I did, everything changed. You could call it magic. It felt like magic". It injected life into his seemingly frail bones, and he began actively participating in all competitions, winning everything he could lay his hands on. 2011 saw a new Djokovic claiming the world of tennis. He was on a winning streak throughout the forty-one straight matches he played before the beginning of the season.

In the same year, he took the bull by the horns, winning against his arch-rivals, Rafael Nadal and Roger Federer. With this, he bagged three majors and five master's titles. Djokovic sealed his place in the world of tennis from 2011 to

2016, pocketing 11 of 24 Grand Slams and taking the keys to the number one spot in the world of tennis every year except in 2013.

Speak your Mind

Can you think of a time when you faced a setback, like losing a big game or not doing well on a test, and how you handled it?

How did it make you feel: giving up or working harder?

Battling Through Losses

Djokovic faced numerous losses early in his career, particularly against rivals Federer and Nadal. However, he used these experiences to strengthen his resolve, eventually surpassing both to become the top-ranked player in the world. Losing is a part of the journey, and every setback is an opportunity to learn, adapt, and return stronger.

MIA HAMM

The year was 1999 at the Orlando Stadium, Florida. It was an international friendly match between the U.S. Women's National Team and Brazil. However, for Mia and the U.S. home crowd, the game was beyond friendly. The determination with which she hunted for the ball, her quick runs, and her acute passes sailing towards the Brazilian goalpost under the efficient paddling of the crowds' cheers showed it was a fight for the birth of history.

The 28th minute of the first half slipped the historic moment into Mia's lethal foot. However, it was not going to be a walk in the park. Before she could aim for the post, she had to contend with two Brazilian honey badgers, who came for a steal. Mia cut through them like a fine butcher in split seconds and edged into the 18-yard box. And that was it. A powerful strike sent the ball soaring into the top far corner of the net like a jet fighter on a mission. It's a goal!!!

Like a storm, Joy uprooted the excited home crowd off their seats; they broke into a symphony of cheers conducted with Mia's name. Overwhelmed, Mia was crumbling to her knees when her rushing teammates took hold of her and buried her in their warm embrace.

She had done it. She had scored her 108th international goal, surpassing Elisabetta Vignotto's record and solidifying her status as the greatest goal-scorer in international soccer history.

Reflecting on the achievement, in an interview after the match, in a voice still glued to heavy emotions, she said, "It's not about the record; it's about the journey and the people who have supported me along the way." This statement mirrors the winding tracks of the supportive people and events on whose back she had ridden over the years to reach that very moment in her life.

Born in the small, quiet town of Selma, Alabama, where everyone knew everyone like the back of their palm, Mia's birth on March 17, 1972, was a joyous event that broke that gentle quietness of the town. With a father, Bill, a proud Air Force pilot who braves the belly of the beast to provide for his home, and a mother, Stephanie, a dedicated homemaker whose watchful eyes watched over Mia and her five siblings and tended the home, Mia didn't have to spend her childhood trying to squeeze joys from rocks.

However, apart from the warmth of a loving family, Mia started the world on the wrong foot. Born with a partial club foot that twisted her feet inwards, imagining a career in football at the time was an imagination stretched too far. It took two years of wearing a cast on her feet before it was successfully corrected.

Even with a cast wrapped around her feet for two years, it didn't trap her passion for soccer. With legs free from the shackles of the cast, Mia would spend hours kicking the ball on the neatly mowed lawn in her backyard with her siblings while their parents watched and cheered them on.

With Mia's ravenous appetite for soccer growing, her parents were quick to fish out her passion for the sport and threw their weight behind her. Unfortunately, their support was a bridge not long enough to cross her over into the world of soccer. This was because, at the time, soccer was not an everyday sport, especially for girls. There weren't any soccer opportunities for girls and women in the United States at that time.

Fortunately for Mia, her passion was a wildfire that circumstances could not quench. With no girls to play with, she played with boys, an experience that tremendously built her confidence, improved her skills, and later gave her an edge over her peers.

Hence, even at a young age, she left an invaluable lesson on the need to work with what we have while waiting for what we desire.

With a passion ready to knock on all doors to succeed, 1978 opened its doors to the six-year-old Mia. It began with the keen eyes of her parents noticing that their quiet hometown, Selma, in Alabama, was no longer enough playground for their daughter's passion. The next stop that came to mind was Wichita Falls, Texas: a city that was not just known for its robust sports culture.

Once in Texas, Mia's passion found a home. She quickly joined the local women's youth soccer club in Wichita Falls. It was here, with an already evident natural talent that needed pruning, that Mia dedicatedly honed her craft under the keen eyes of a coach. Mia didn't take long to become a phenom in the local league. She showed exceptional talent and skill that edge ahead of her peers.

At age 14, Mia's journey into the world of soccer took a major leap. She joined an Olympic Development Team based in Dallas. Dallas was the scaffold Mia needed to climb into the world of professional football.

A year in the team was enough for Mia to prove herself in the team. With her magnetic dribbling skills and fast footwork, she was quick to pull the attention of Coach Anson Dorrance, renowned coach of the U.S. women's national team and the University of North Carolina's women's soccer team. This moment swung open the door to an illustrious career.

It began with an invitation from Coach Dorrance in 1987, which walked Mia into the U.S. national team. This hung her name on the wall of history books as the youngest player ever to play for the U.S. national team.

Two years after she joined the national team, in 1989, Coach Dorrance guided Mia to join the University of North Carolina at Chapel. She was young but fiercely talented, 17 years old. Mia came as a piping red hot soldering iron; she melted everything into a trophy.

Starting in 1989, when she joined the North Carolina Tar Heels women's soccer team, she went on a rampage with them. They won the NCAA Women's Championships on a four streak from 1989 to 1992. What better way again does one announce excellence?

However, Mia was not the favorite kid in soccer to have gone on a streak without the bruises of setbacks. Early 1991 was a beautiful year that opened to the windmill arms of Mia's excellence hovering over the sky of the University of North Carolina's soccer team until April 14, 1991, when a thunderbolt of tragedy shot her off its sky.

It happened during a fierce match against the University of Connecticut. A collision with a Connecticut defender crippled her to the ground in an unbearable pain. She quickly discovered she had been handed a broken leg, a devastating injury that eclipsed her for the rest of the season.

The road to recovery was not a walk to MacDonalds for pizza. It was tough. Mia underwent surgery, with months of intense rehabilitation coming on its heels. However, for one whose passion for the game grew even when cast shackled her clubfoot for two years, a broken leg of a few months does not have enough muscles to steal her passion.

At the end of the year, Mia's vibrant legs were tucked into her boots. She was pivotal in the U.S. Women's National Team's World Cup campaign held in China. This groundbreaking event was significant in women's soccer as it was the first-ever FIFA Women's World Cup.

From the first match in the tournament, Mia was an ivory tour, and crowds of attention nestled on her. Her incredible ability to seamlessly weave through colonies of defenders and set up scoring opportunities made her an invaluable asset to her team.

In the knockout stages, Mia was a live wire. She netted key goals, gave assists, and shouldered the U.S. team to secure their place in history as the first women's soccer team to win Olympic gold. It also etched Mia's name in history as the youngest player in that tournament.

In 1996, twenty-four-year-old Mia walked and announced herself at the Atlanta Olympics with her trademark of excellence. She poured her passion and brilliance into the tournament. A feat that launched her to the peak of her career.

In 1997, Mia was at the peak of her career, still basking in the euphoria of her tremendous show at the Olympics. While still caught up in her win, a tragic knock came unannounced at her doorstep and tucked her into grief. It happened on April 16, 1997, when she received the news that her brother, Garrett, had passed away due to complications from aplastic anemia, a rare blood disease.

The news bore a hole in Mia's heart and crumpled her into a mammoth of grief. Mia had a special relationship with her brother, Garrett. He was his cheerleader: a source of strength and inspiration. His death was a brutal hit on her. Completely overwhelmed with grief, she struggled to come to terms with his loss. The grief momentarily quenched her passion for the one thing she had loved all her life - soccer.

It took the determined efforts of her family and teammates to get her ready on her wings to fly again. Although her brother was dead, she didn't want his memory to lose breath as he did. This inspired her decision to honor his memory.

She put her grief into action by establishing the Mia Hamm Foundation, dedicated to bone marrow research and providing opportunities for young athletes. Transforming her tragedy into positive action leaves an invaluable lesson on perseverance and the determination to find a silver lining in the sky no matter how gloomy the clouds get.

With grief behind her, she waltzed into the summer of 1999 as a beacon of hope for the U.S. Women's National Team as they competed in the FIFA Women's World Cup. One of her outstanding moments came during the semifinal against Brazil, where her precise assist led to a crucial goal, propelling the team to the final.

The daybreak of a new millennium woke up to an already set Mia. The U.S. team rode on the back of her role as an expert playmaker and an exceptional forward to the finals of the Sydney Olympics in 2000. Although they narrowly shied away from victory following a defeat by Norway, Mia's presence was inspirational to the younger players in the team.

With her career itching to an end, Mia wouldn't bow out of the stage without having a gold medal dangled down her neck. So, when she arrived at the 2004 Olympics in Athens, she knew it would be her last. She was set to pour blood and sweat into it. With eyes brimming with hunger and passion, she pulled the team to their final against a tough Brazilian team in the U.S. on August 26, 2004.

The match was a clash of rocks bruising both teams. However, in a match that dangled on the unsteady rope of heart-wrenching plot twists and heavy tension, Mia came to the rescue in the extra time, contributing significantly to her team's hard-fought 2-1 victory. With this win, she bowed out of the global stage in high spirits.

She finally drew the curtain on an illustrious career of seventeen years after participating in a farewell match by the U.S. Women's National Team. Standing on the big stage, she took a bow with 158 international goals, two World Cup titles, and two Olympic gold medals, retiring as one of the most celebrated athletes in soccer history.

Speak your Mind

Can you think of a time when you had to adjust to a new situation, like starting a new school, moving to a different neighborhood, switching positions on your sports team, or learning a new way to solve a math problem?

How did the change make you feel? Was it easy for you to adapt to the change? Did adapting to that change help you succeed or fail in what you were doing?

Adaptability is the Key to Unlock Opportunities

Adapting to change can be challenging but also a powerful way to grow. Take Mia Hamm, for example. When she was young, her family moved often because her father was in the military. Each new place meant new schools, new friends, and new challenges. However, Mia used these changes as opportunities to improve her soccer skills and learn from different coaches.

LISA LESLIE

Pressure stood tall on the back of the US women's national basketball team on the night of August 4, 1996, at the Atlanta Olympics. Having lost its birthright of clinching gold in the Olympics after its 1988 Olympics, finishing third place in the 1992 Olympics and 1994 World Championships, the 1996 Summer Olympics was not just a game.

It was America fighting to claim its place as king in basketball. With an already impressive win in their last seven games, which has given them a place in tonight's final against Brazil, they could feel the victory in sight.

But anxiety weighed in their hearts like a heavy rock. It wasn't just because they were playing against the Brazilian magic team, but also because the 32,997

American fans with their hearts on their sleeves had come to watch them take back what 'rightfully belonged to them.'

The name, "Lisa Leslie," was a chorus playing on the hopeful lips of the excited fans. Her raised hand stood solidly upright against the pushes and shoves of the Brazilian defense line and was the trusted powerline the team needed to make a solid connection to victory. She shouldered the burden of expectations. She had incredible strength that was not born solely from lifting weights, pushups, and sit-ups.

Before continuing this story, let's time-travel back to Lisa Leslie's early life to discover how she grew so tall and developed powerful basketball skills.

Born on July 7, 1972, in the Compton section of Los Angeles, USA, to a father who is a professional basketballer and to her mother Christine Leslie. Lisa Leslie's father deserted the family when she was four, and the mother took up the job of cross-country truck driver because she wanted to take care of Lisa and her two older sisters.

Lisa spent most of her school year with her aunt or a babysitter. During summer, she and her sisters supported their mother by accompanying her on cross-country driving. During this period, they slept in the back of the truck. This was Lisa's first major life challenge.

This experience was hard enough to toughen any child. Of course, it didn't leave Lisa behind. But her wall of confidence began to crack in elementary school. Having the genes of a father who has the athletic build of a professional basketballer and her mother who stands 6.3 in her body, it was not surprising when, at elementary school, she already dwarfed her teacher with her then 5.2 height. But her classmates and other pupils were not having it. Soon, her height began to receive a bouquet of mockery.

She commented, "They called me Olive Oyl; they called me all sorts of things." This dug a hole in her confidence and self-esteem. It took her mother's intervention to learn how to accept herself and love her stature.

Seeing Lisa's impressive height, the first thing that springs to mind is basketball. However, Lisa was not interested in the game of loop for one bit.

The more people asked her, "Do you play basketball?" instead of inspiring her to try the game, she hated it. But standing six feet tall in seventh grade, her middle school classmates and friends couldn't imagine her doing anything with such an impressive height but basketball.

They always pushed, prodded, and begged her to join the school team. Finally, to free herself from the constant pestering, she decided to join.

At first, when she joined the team, playing was a chore. She had little or no interest. In an interview years later, she said, "All I did was to be tall, they'd just throw the ball at me, and I'd make the basket….All I did was do what I was told". Despite her unenthusiasm, her presence on the court was enough to make her middle school team go undefeated that year.

Perhaps it was part of something beautiful, being associated with a team that flickered a budding flame of interest that would later grow into a wildfire of passion that would consume her.

The spark came to life when, after middle school, she moved in with an aunt. Her aunt's home was the incubation period. Living under the same roof with a male older cousin, a basketballer, Lisa fell in love with the game. Her older cousin became her private coach. With the daily routine exercises he gave her, Lisa honed her skills and strengthened her lanky bones.

During this time, she played with predominantly male teams, which not only built her confidence but also brought out the star in her.

As a freshman at Morningside High School in Inglewood, Lisa's exceptional skills were evident. She bore the imprints of her cousin's mentorship. She was a magnet that pulled the attention of basketball lovers even to the national level. She averaged 21.7 points, 12.8 rebounds, and 6.2 blocks that year. Her impressive feat caught the admiration of USA Today, which named her a first-team high school All-American.

A new Lisa walked down the courts of Morningside High School the following season. The new Lisa showed her new self in one of her unforgettable high school games. It was a match against South Torrance. In the first half of the game, Lisa was a whirlwind. In sixteen minutes, she singlehandedly clinched

101 points. The first half ended on 102-24. With thirty-one free throws and thirty-seven field goals in the first half, she made a national high school record.

Lisa waited for the second half of the game to break the record held by basketball legend Cheryl Miller for points in a single. But the Torrance coach, with the weight of humiliation of the first half still hanging heavily on his neck, decided to call it quits before the second half, thereby denying Lisa the chance.

Although this was a painful experience for Lisa, the game was a significant turning point in her fortune in the game. It got her a lot of attention, and even before she graduated, she received loads of letters from different universities calling her to come to their schools. Lisa earned the Naismith Award, the Dial Award for the nation's top high school student-athlete, and a new state record of 1705 rebounds at Morningside High School.

With lots of invites from different universities after high school, which made her the most recruited female basketball player since Miller in 1983, Lisa was confused. However, to stay closer to her home, she finally chose the University of Southern California (USC), which happened to be the Legend Miller alma mater. It is here that she shot herself to the limelight.

At USC, Lisa was a force. She took hold of every award she could lay her hands on. As a freshman, her exceptional skills were so evident that from 1990 to 1994, during her stay at USC, she constantly earned a place on the Pac-10 first team. With this, she made history as the first Freshman to be named to the Pac-10 team.

Singlehandedly, she championed the team to four NCAA, and in 1992 and 1994, she stole them a place in the "Great Eight." But this was just the tip of the iceberg. During her senior season, she averaged 21.9 points and 12.3 rebounds per game, earning a second Naismith Award. Between 1992 and 1994, she was named an All-American. To crown it all, in 1993, the USA Basketball named her Female Athlete of the Year.

By the time Lisa graduated in 1994, basketball was no longer just a school sport; it was something she wanted to spend her life doing. During this time, female basketball at a professional level has not become such a huge thing. Most U.S. female professional players played professionally in countries like Brazil, Spain, and Japan.

This forced Lisa to travel to Sicilgesso, Italy, to play professionally. But she could play for only a season before 1995; in the build-up to the Atlanta Olympics, she decided to try out for the U.S. national team. Of course, her impressive records earned her a place on the team.

In the buildup to the Olympics, Lisa took her preparation personally. This was because, during the team's pre-Olympic tour, where the team played against the best international and top U.S. college teams, Lisa discovered that her height was not enough. Her slender frame made it easy for the opposing defenses to take her out of the game, weakening her team.

Speaking on this in the New York Times, she said. "Their strategy is to beat me up, get me out of the game." This affected her game as she only averaged 17.3 points and seven rebounds per game during the tour. The one lesson here is that success is a journey of steady improvement.

Conscious of the magic she could unleash with her height if she was much stronger, instead of merely wishing, she got to work. She worked out, lifting just enough weight to clothe herself with stamina. This toughened her up and birthed her aggressive style of play, which breaks down the pillar of every defense line each time she steps onto the court. This was Lisa, who had walked on the Olympic court in Atlanta in 1996.

This will help you better understand the charged atmosphere described earlier at the story's beginning. It will also help you understand why the 32,977 U.S. basketball fans who gathered on the night of August 4, 1996, for the final match between the U.S. and Brazil had the name Lisa Leslie on their lips.

Lisa didn't disappoint. She shouldered the expectations. In a match that would end with the scoreline 111-87 in favor of the U.S., Lisa rose to the occasion, leading her team with 29 points and six rebounds, clinching the much-coveted gold medal.

However, Lisa's story does not begin and end with basketball or the Olympics. Apart from being a legendary athlete, she had eyes for modeling. This dream came to life after the Olympics. Although she had intended to try out a new women's professional League Basketball, the American Basketball League, she decided to take leave of basketball for a while.

It was here she dove into modeling with a contract with the US top Modelling Agency, Wilhelmina. This ushered her into print and runway modeling. She modeled sportswear on Vogue, TV Guide, and Shape pages.

In an interview with Women's Sports and Fitness, she spoke on handling both careers and said, "I'm passionate about both, and when I'm doing both, I'm giving you me." Going further, she said, "I'm being aggressive, doing what I love and what I've practiced with attitude and style, The big difference is, I'm showered and clean when I'm modeling. The point is, I am a woman, always." With this, Lisa defied the stereotype that a female athlete should appear manly.

For Lisa, athleticism does not take away girliness or is not an excuse for not being feminine. This is why, even on or off the court, one cannot fail to notice her poise and elegance in how she carries herself and how she dresses up whenever she is representing the U.S. team.

Basketball called Lisa again in December 1996. This was during the build-up of what would be today known as the Women's National Basketball Association (WNBA), an extension of the NBA. She became one of the league's pioneer players. She played for the Los Angeles Sparks, a team in her hometown.

She started as one of its pioneer players in June 1997. She spent the rest of her basketball career here until 2009, when she retired with a record as the leading scorer and rebounder. She also became a part owner of Sparks.

Lisa did an excellent job combining her basketball and modeling careers. She would later explore the world of broadcasting, putting her degree in communications to good use.

Lisa's life is an inspiration and a true testament that with dedication and strong faith, one can be a Jack of all trades and master of all. Her concluding remarks in her interview with Women's Sports and Fitness summarize it all: "You can be whatever you want to be. Women don't have to fulfill the stereotype of looking like men with their clothes hanging off them just because they play basketball,".

Speak your Mind

Can you think of a time when someone made fun of you for something unique about you, like wearing glasses, being tall or short, being left-handed, speaking with an accent, having a unique way of thinking, or having an exceptional talent?

How do you think you could use that unique trait to achieve something amazing in your life, like how wearing glasses can help you read and learn more efficiently to become a top student or how people with unique ways of thinking can become great inventors or problem solvers?

Taking Advantage of Your Uniqueness

Everyone has something unique about them, and sometimes people might make fun of it. But you can turn that uniqueness into your strength! Here's how:

Identify Your Strength: Consider what makes you unique and how it can be useful.

Research and Learn: Find out how others with similar traits have succeeded.

Practice and Improve: Work on developing your unique ability.

Stay Confident: Believe in yourself and your uniqueness.

Showcase Your Talent: Use your unique trait to excel in activities you love.

By following these steps, you can turn what others might tease you about into something that helps you achieve your goals!

KATIE LEDECKY

Katie, one of the best Olympic swimmers America has ever known, was experiencing an emotion she had never felt before gliding into her heart. Only that this time, it was not love but fear: fear that her windmill arms were about to fail her yet again. Not so long ago, it had failed her once in her 400-metre freestyle opening race, where for the first time in her three-time appearance in the race, she finished second behind Australian Ariarne Titmus. Now, in a 200-metre rematch with Ariarne, she won't let her leave the pool again with the gold.

For a moment, she feared she might rip her shoulders apart if she pushed any harder through the water. She was not used to struggling to win. Locked in her thoughts, she heard the hurricane hands of the 20-year-old Ariane edging past her once again to another gold. Her heart tightened at the thought of that. But Ariane reminded her of her 20-year-old self at the 2016 Olympics, and she imagined what the older athletes must have felt when she beat them to their race.

Before she dazzled the world in Rio 2016 and is struggling now with Tokyo 2020, Katie's life and journey into the world of the swimming pool are fascinating and inspiring. Although Katie Ledecky grew up in Bethesda, Maryland, her interesting life journey started close to the residence of the United States President in Washington, D.C., where she was born on March 17, 1997, to her dad, David Ledecky, and her mom, Mary Gen Ledecky.

Katie didn't spend forever to find her passion; it was an open door that had been there waiting for her just to stroll in. Growing up in a family atmosphere where passion for profession and love of fun burnt: with an attorney dad, a one-time collegiate swimmer mom, and a pool-loving elder brother, Michael, Katie found her way to the pool pretty fast. It was her favorite fun activity.

In 2003, at age six, with the support of her mom, Katie and her brother began competitive swimming at the Palisades Swim & Tennis Club. Here, she began to build the strength of her windmill arms to paddle her into an illustrious career.

At 14, under the special guidance of coach Yuri Sugiyama, she became a sensation. The coach took a special interest in Katie because of her budding magical swimming skills. Seeing her elite potential, the coach began coaching her on how to kick her legs more aggressively underwater while racing. This technique was not much practiced in women's swimming; it was particularly common among elite male swimmers.

This practice put her miles ahead of her peers and built enormous strength into her arms and legs, which in turn built her incredible trademark endurance in mid and long-distance swimming.

Katie's incredible skill and endurance first came to life in the summer of 2011, before her freshman year at high school. It was during the U.S. Junior Championships. She announced her presence with the ease with which she dominated the long and mid-distance swimming: 1,500, 800, and 400-meter swimming freestyle events.

Her impressive run pushed her and gave her the confidence that launched her into the senior national team. She made her senior national team debut in the U.S. Olympics Trials in 2012, opting for the 200, 400, and 800-metre swimming freestyles.

Standing against top-level athletes in the trial, who weren't particularly bothered about her presence in the race just like they weren't of other new timers, she wasn't intimidated for a second. She showed her mettle in the 800-meter freestyle, where she beat everyone to it and sailed herself a spot in the London 2012 Olympic Team as the youngest person across all sports.

London Olympics 2012 watched the confident 15-year-old high school freshman shoot herself into the world stage. She was never the one to be star-struck. She came to the global stage to write her name in block letters; there was no room for intimidation.

With an impressive run that took her to the finals of the 800-meter race, she did write her name in the sands of time: surging out of the pool in a time record of 8 minutes 14.63 seconds to break the American record of Janet and claim the gold.

Speaking on her win, she said, "I knew if I put my mind to it, I could do it…I wasn't intimidated at all." Katie's mentality teaches us to believe in ourselves. Apart from her excellent skill, her belief and confidence in herself gave her the courage to be in tune with herself and give an ace performance even though she competed against top athletes.

Katie's mentality leaves an invaluable lesson for everyone: skills are not enough; you must have the confidence to show them off on whatever stage the occasion calls excellently.

At the end of the London Olympics, Katie Ledecky had become a household name. She went ahead to prove that her landmark on the world stage wasn't a flash in the pan. It was confidence, skill, and hard work. So, in the build-up to the World Aquatics Championships (former FINA World Championships) in 2013, she established world records by wrapping her arms tightly around the 800 and 1,500-metre freestyle swimming.

She clinched four golds at the competition. In 2014 and 2015, she did it again, clinching four golds at the Pan Pacific Swimming Championships and the World Championships. With this, she became the first woman in a major competition to win the mid and long-distance races: 200, 400, 800, and 1,500-metre freestyle. She did not just take the titles; she did it with wide margins between her and her competitors.

With her incredible feats, her global recognition soared: she was a nine-time Golden Goggle Female Athlete of the Year, a three-time U.S. Olympic Committee's Female Olympic Athlete of the Year, and a two-time Swimmer of the Year honor by FINA and World Aquatics.

In between the years, precisely in 2015, her impressive records fetched her a spot in athletic scholarship, even before she graduated from high school at one of the most sought-after U.S. universities, Stanford. This shows that despite her career success, she was still interested in a sound education.

Leaving her soaring swimming career to further her education was a callous decision. The admission had come during the buildup for the Rio de Janeiro Olympics. With the high rate of rejections that came at the heels of hundreds of people who apply for admission at Stanford each year, she knew Standford was not a school anyone could afford to keep waiting. So, she was torn between taking up her admission or going in for the Rio Olympics, an opportunity that may come ever again.

After much back-and-forth, she made the challenging decision to defer her admission to focus her full attention on her training. In this decision, she reveals a fundamental secret to her success: goal setting. She gives things adequate attention and does them properly rather than juggling them only to mess them up.

By giving herself adequate time to focus on the Olympic preparations, the 2016 Olympics found her in the finest forms. At the Arena Pro Swim Series, in full glare of the world's admiration, her 18-year-old fully blown windmill arms, bustling with the easy confidence of one who was not afraid to announce her presence on the highest stage, set her 11th world record. She won her 800-meter freestyle in a record 8 minutes 6.68 seconds.

At the end of her impressive run at Rio de Janeiro, elegantly standing undefeated in all major international competitions and retaining her world record in 400 and 1,500-meter freestyle titles, she walled herself into the corridors of the American team's most celebrated Olympian.

With eight years lying between the London 2012 Olympics, when she was just a teen who walked onto the world stage and etched her name in gold, and the 2020 Tokyo Olympics, when she had become a full-blown adult with more experience, surprisingly, Katie faced a challenge that was alien to her.

The 2020 Tokyo Olympics was a different ball game. She was 24. There were younger and faster swimmers. Having lost the 400-meter freestyle to a much younger Ariarne for the very first time in her pro career in her opening race and with heavy arms that might as well fail her yet again in the 200-meter race, it was the knowledge of these losses that buried Katie in all the emotions and thoughts that we witnessed at the beginning of this story.

Now, let's continue with her 2020 Tokyo Olympics story that we started in the beginning. She was still submerged in the pool and wouldn't stop hearing the sound of the fiery arms of other swimmers paddling past her. She could eavesdrop on the doubts in the unusual silence that hung over the pool like a dark cloud. This was followed immediately by the sound splash of the weight of expectations of her fans collapsing on her back, pressing her down, and choking her.

But in a tournament where she had seen athletes like Simon Biles and Naomi Osaka crumble under the weight of personal and general expectations on their long history of excellence, the burden of expectations was not what she wanted for herself.

Quickly, she pushed herself forward, removing herself from the weight, ignoring the groans of her arms. When she uprooted her head from the water, she saw the number 5 attached to her name. She had just graced her worst finish and the most challenging day of her swimming career.

Although tears welled in her eyes, her dark goggles didn't let them see the light of the day. It was an unbelievable moment. But she didn't spend time crying over spilled milk by dwelling on the negatives. She went on to practice for her 1,500-meter freestyle to see how she could improve.

This attitude towards her setback reflects the core of the fundamental beliefs that have guided her throughout her career. In her words, "Always try to be moving forward, don't dwell on failures and disappointments, just try to find positives in everything you do and find things that you are passionate about. Try to be the best you can be. I think if you are always striving at self-improvement then that's the best you can do, and always try to find positives in hard moments, I think that's the most important thing". This is the best attitude for anyone in the journey of success.

While Katie nursed her bruises, she trained still. By the time she was submerged in the pool again for the 1,500-meter freestyle, her mind wandered to everything and finally rested on her grandparents, whom she was very fond of. Thinking about them made her strong. Speaking later on about this, Katie said, "They are four of the toughest people I know. I knew if I was thinking about them during the race, I wasn't going to die (swimming slang for tiring out at the end), and I wasn't going to have a bad race". Although she was tiring out, she soldiered on.

At the elapse of 15 minutes, 37.34 seconds, tired and worn out, Katie's head burst out of the water. Pulling her goggles to her head, she saw the number 1 sitting prettily beside her name. She had won the race.

At this moment, her heart cranked open, and the visibly emotional Katie let out a scream that calibrated every inch of frustration and despair she had felt throughout the uneventful games: a scream that cut into the loud celebrations and cheers going on in the jubilant American section of the arena.

Although the win was behind the record she set in previous Olympics, it was a win she desperately needed so badly to reassure herself.

After her win, she said, "The times might not be my best times, but I'm still very happy that I have a gold medal around my neck right now." She said these words with quivering lips and eyes ripe with joyful tears. Still motivated by her victory, she went on to clinch another gold and a silver at the 800-meter freestyle and 4x100 relay race.

Immediately after the Tokyo Olympics, with the mind of one unwilling to get herself in a difficult moment that would weigh on her, she moved to Gainsville, Florida, to focus solely on her training. There, together with other Olympic swimmers, she trained under the head coach Anthony Nesty.

Fast-forward to the build-up to the Paris Olympics 2024. She has once more spread her wings in the U.S. Olympic Swimming Team Trials, where she won all four events: a testament to her strength and dedication. By the end of the Olympics, she will have become a living legend in the sport and a model for anyone committed to a journey of success.

Speak your Mind

Can you think of a time in sports, like during a soccer match or basketball game, when you faced a challenging situation or made a mistake?

How did you move forward and find something positive to focus on, like Katie Ledecky thinking about how tough her grandparents were after a failure or disappointment?

Did improving your skills and remembering past successes help you get better and enjoy the game more?

Focusing on the positive after failures and disappointments

Focusing on the positive after failures and disappointments is a powerful way to keep moving forward. Take Katie Ledecky, for example. After experiencing setbacks in her swimming career, she would think about how tough her grandparents were and use that as motivation. This helped her stay positive and continue striving for success.

In your everyday life, you can also take away positives from failures and disappointments. If you didn't win a race, think about how much faster you've become and how you can train even better next time. If you made a mistake in a game, focus on what you learned and how it will help you improve. Remember, every setback is an opportunity to learn and grow. Keep your passion alive, and always strive to be your best!

JERRY RICE

The Mississippi sun has an ongoing dialogue with the Earth. It positioned itself closer, like an old friend leaning in. One could feel its warmth at B.L. Moore High School as the sun's fierce rays intensified, evaporating the river of sweat from the students in the classrooms. One student was uncomfortable learning in the heat; He wanted to be anywhere but not in the classroom.

He was the student who would go on to become one of the greatest wide receivers in the history of American football. To escape the torture, he did the only thing that came to his mind: sneak out of the class. Little did he know that it was fate calling him. A surprise awaited him at a bend in the long corridor.

As he tiptoed away, his eyes ran through the empty corridor. Making sure that the eagle eyes of his teachers were not looking, he heard familiar echoes of footsteps. He was almost face-to-face with the assistant principal. Before his mind decided to do the only wise thing there was to do: turn back and run.

He took off at a jet-like speed, allowing the assistant principal only a glimpse of his billowing red jacket. The assistant principal was stunned. His anger at the truancy was quickly replaced by amazement at the swiftness with which the student's legs had eaten up the floor. "Anyone who can run that fast should be playing sports," he thought.

Still, the assistant principal recognized the student even in his speed. This made it easy to fish him out for a disciplinary measure the following day. However, the assistant principal's action after the disciplinary measure would change the course of the student's life.

The speed that swept the student out of his sight in a flash was still a marvel to him. After the disciplinary measure, he took him to the school football coach to have him make good use of his legs on the team. This incident led to the birth of the household name Jerry Rice, widely recognized as the National Football League's greatest wide receiver of all time.

Jerry Lee Rice was born in the predominantly poor black neighborhood of Crawford in Starkville, Mississippi, on October 13, 1962. Although the poor neighborhood had nothing much to give, it didn't steal joy from Jerry's childhood.

Born into a family of eight to a hardworking bricklayer father who engaged the services of Jerry and his brothers during the blazingly hot Southern Summers, Jerry not only squeezed out peals of laughter that cemented their family bond, but he also took life lessons that would later lead him to a successful career. Speaking on the experience in retrospect, he'd say, "It taught me the meaning of hard work."

Football was not one of the things Jerry ever imagined he'd spend his life doing. He didn't learn about football until his second year in high school. But before the incredible speed of his legs led him into the school football team, the ordinary activities of his everyday life in his obscure neighborhood had inadvertently prepared him for a footballing career. This included frequent, endless runs across his neighborhood's sharp bends and curves. He practically ran a distance of five miles to and fro school, which strengthened his legs for what lay ahead of him.

Secondly, tossing and catching bricks on a scaffold almost every other hour, when he and his brothers helped out their father in his work, gave him rock-solid and sensitive hands. Recalling this youth activity, he said, "One of my brothers would stack about four bricks on each other and toss them up. I would catch all four. I did it so many times; it was just a reaction." These experiences made playing the role of a wide receiver in football come naturally to him.

In Jerry's second year at B.L. Moor High School in Crawford, his high school coach handed him pads and made him queue in as a receiver. Although he had no experience in playing football, he was quick to learn and developed at a breakneck pace that surprised everyone.

It did not take long before he became a formidable offensive threat for the team. Towards the end of his high school career, football became not just a sport but a passion he was obsessed with and would love to spend his life playing.

However, his first challenge was getting into a major college. This was the first significant setback to his dreams. Even with his impressive high school records, Jerry's background greatly hindered his career.

With his school located in a poor neighborhood populated mainly by African Americans, it had a negative reputation that nothing good could come out of it. College coaches scouting for players avoided the area. This made it difficult for Jerry to get into any major college on a scholarship as he would have loved to.

The only scholarship offer was from Mississippi Valley State University. Although the school's reputation was not much better than that of his high school, Jerry just needed a 'yes' to have the opportunity to prove himself.

So, he grabbed the offer with both hands, hoping that if he proved himself there, he'd get better offers. This experience teaches us an invaluable lesson:

in the journey to success, we must start working with what is before us while waiting for what we eventually want.

This was precisely what he did. He joined the small school in the predominantly Black area, which had barely two thousand enrollments. Jerry's coach, Archie Cooley, had so much faith in his potential. He wanted him to play a crucial role in the team.

So, he introduced a completely new offense style called "the spread" when he brought Jerry into the Delta Devils team. This new pattern closely resembles the fast break in basketball and involves lots of passes. This made enough room for Jerry's incredible receiving ability to shine out.

This new pattern worked out perfectly for the Delta Devils. They averaged 61 points per game, and Jerry wore his wide receiver role well. In four seasons, Jerry had 4,693 yards receiving, finishing with 18 Division 1-AA records. He set an NCAA all-division record by catching twenty-four passes in a game.

By his senior year, with a hunger for success and the desire to prove that he was worth more than the picture his immediate environment paints of him, he set all kinds of NCAA records. As a senior, he singlehandedly caught one hundred and twelve passes for 1,845 yards and scored twenty-eight touchdowns. All this climaxed in the Freedom Bowl All-Star game, where he finished as the Most Valuable Player of the game.

By the end of college, Jerry had become an incredible player. News of his exceptional catching and scoring skills, which projected him as the best wide receiver, had made it around the small town. Local television carried news of his exploits.

One would expect that with this newfound fame, scouters would scramble for Jerry, but it was still the same old story. The National Football League teams (NFL) had low regard for colleges that played under the Southwestern Athletic Conference. They considered their pattern of play dubious and unrealistic. They also did not trust the strength of the coaching there. So, they were unconvinced Jerry had what it took to go pro.

This cast a long dark shadow on Jerry's chances of ever going pro, as these teams didn't cast him at the top of their draft list, while others didn't cast him at all.

The gloomy cloud began to disperse on a night in 1985 when the head coach of the San Francisco 49ers, Bill Walsh, came across the news of Jerry's exceptional skills. It was a night before his team's away match with the Houston Oilers.

His attention was caught by the local news announcer, who continuously displayed highlights of the incredible swift scoring of Jerry in a match against the University of Houston. Watching the then '23-year-old wide receiver weave through the defense line, Walsh knew he had found an engine for his team's offense line.

Trusting Jerry's potential to improve their team, the head coach of the San Francisco 49ers decided to take him with the 16th selection in the 1985 draft. This was Jerry's break. But most of the San Francisco 49ers fans did not have it. Questions like, "Who is Jerry? Where is he from?" which announced their doubt of his ability, kept pouring in. Jerry needed no soothsayer to tell him he had only one assignment in the team: to prove himself.

Jerry's first season with the 49ers wasn't an easy ride. The complicated offense line of the team was a hard nut to crack. The offense style was completely new to him. It didn't give him room to play naturally. In his words, "I was thinking through every step of a complicated offense." He struggled to adapt to the pattern. It showed in matches where his magnetic hands were constantly dropping the ball. This confirmed the tight-bow doubts of the fans that clutched his neck since he joined the team.

But his coach, Bill Walsh, was a patient man. He had so much faith in him even when the fans had none. This was the only light he needed to pull out of the dark tunnel. He put in the work. It was here that his incredible, legendary work ethic came to life.

He worked out six days a week. He did two hours of cardiovascular training in the morning: running up a huge hill and finishing by sprinting through the hill's most steep part. Then, in the afternoon, he did three hours of strength training.

He kept strictly to this routine, a significant lesson that talent and skill are not enough. They must be backed up by hard work, discipline, and a strong mindset.

1986 saw a new Jerry emerge in the blue-grey leather game. It was the year he began writing his name eternally into the history of American football. He dominated the league, making 86 catches, 1570 yards, and 15 touchdowns.

By 1987, Jerry had become a sensation. He scored a league-high 23 touchdowns, setting a new league record. A feat that earned him his first NFL Player of the Year. In the 1988-1989 season, with 11 catches and 205 yards, which saw the 49ers defeat the Bengals 20-16, Jerry clinched Super Bowl XXIII and the MVP of the game.

By 1987, the name of the boy from the poor Crawford neighborhood, previously caged within the environs of Mississippi, became a national sensation everyone wanted to associate with. He was invited for interviews and had to speak before large audiences. A testament to his fame.

However, he had a major challenge: He had trouble speaking to large audiences. After a few fumbles while speaking before large audiences, he knew public speaking was something he had to learn. So, he hired a speech coach. He said, "I needed somebody to smooth out my speech." This particular act of Jerry teaches one crucial lesson: the need for constant self-improvement in all aspects of life.

Self-improvement was the hallmark of Jerry's career. Even as the years went on and he became established as the best wide receiver in the sport, with nothing much left to improve about his game, which was already at its peak, he never let go of his work ethic and strict diet. He was known for his top fitness level.

In twenty NFL seasons, Jerry never missed a game at any level. Only in 1997, after two severe knee injuries, he was forced to miss 14 games. He simply was not a man to give excuses.

At the end of his twenty-year illustrious career, Jerry had made a name for himself as the GOAT in wide receiving. He pocketed 38 NFL records, such as a staggering 1,549 career receptions, 22,895 receiving yards, 197 touchdowns, etc. He won three Super Bowl rings with the 49ers.

He was named a member of the NFL All-Decades Teams of 1980 and 1990s and the league's 75th-anniversary team. In 2010, he was inducted into the Professional Football Hall of Fame.

Since his break in 1987 until his retirement in 2005, Jerry has set and broken almost every record in the world of American football, a testament to his dedication and hard work. In a press conference where he announced his retirement, he noted, "I have pushed my body for 20 years. I was never a couch potato; I was always working out. I had to prove myself every year."

Surprisingly, with all his achievements, Jerry doesn't just want his name in the history books because of his accomplishments. In his words, "To me, it was never about what I accomplished on the football field. It was about the way I played the game". It was not just about the records but his discipline, his attention to the tiny details, his work ethic, and his desire to be a role model and inspiration to others. Jerry's life is a handbook for anyone who wishes to succeed. It tells one story: no shortcuts or excuses exist for one who truly wants to succeed.

Speak your Mind

Can you think of any skills or experiences you've gained from one activity, like playing a musical instrument or participating in sports, that you've found helpful in other parts of your life?

For example, how has teamwork in soccer helped you work better on school projects?

Or how has the discipline you learned in practicing piano helped you stay focused on your homework?

Or how has the patience you learned from caring for a pet helped you stay calm under pressure during exams?

Every Experience and Skill in Life Counts

Jerry Rice, a legendary football player, learned valuable skills by catching stacks of bricks from his brother. This improved his hand-eye coordination and concentration, which later helped him become one of the best receivers in football history. Like Jerry, you can use skills from one area of life in another. For instance, teamwork in sports can help you with group projects at school, and the patience you develop while learning an instrument can help you stay focused during exams.

CARL LEWIS

Carl could see the cloud of confusion gathering like a storm in the widening eyes of the sympathizers who had come to bid their final farewell to his father. He could eavesdrop on the echo of questions their confusion raised, splitting their mournful lips. The stares sitting in their widened gaze were not the surprise of seeing that after a strenuous fight with cancer, his father, Lewis, seemed so much alive in the casket, but a different kind of surprise.

He saw the shock waken in the tear-rimmed eyes of his mom, Evelyn. He knew the question that look carried even without her saying a word. He had placed the first-ever gold medal he won in a 100-meter race at the 1984 Los Angeles Olympics in the cold, lifeless hand of his father, to be buried with him.

"Don't worry, I will get another one," he promised his mother, who didn't seem to make sense of the gesture, with the easy confidence of one who had become accustomed to winning. This drama played out in Birmingham, Alabama, in 1987.

This promise and the desire to immortalize his father became the fuel that would burn in his heart in the 1988 Olympics in Seoul, South Korea. In his words, "A lot happened to me last year, especially the death of my father. That caused me to re-educate myself to be the very best I possibly can be this season,". Carl came into the 1988 Olympics with the hunger to fulfill a promise. However, the atmosphere on the Seoul cloud did not promise an easy ride.

With the presence of athletes new and old athletes who have feats to achieve and broken egos to mend, 1988 was different from the 1984 games, where Carl entered four events and went ahead to pocket all the golds with ease. In Seoul, he entered for the same events: the long jump, 100m, 200m, and 4x100 relay race. But despite his best efforts, the odds were not in his favor.

First, he finished second in the 100m race, where he had claimed a gold medal four years before. He lost it to his Canadian archrival, Ben Johnson, who finished at 9.79 seconds, a new world record ahead of his 9. 92 seconds' American record. With that win, Carl lost the chance to fulfill his promise of getting another gold in place of the one buried with his father.

But Seoul still held surprises for him. In the 200m, Carl trailed behind Joe Deloach, who set a new Olympic record by finishing in 19.75 seconds. The 4x100 relay race was a disastrous outing for the American team. A fumble in the heat of baton exchange got them disqualified.

The defeats were like heavy loads pressing down Carl's shoulders. However, it didn't have enough grips to keep him underwater during the long jump, where he leaped a low-altitude Olympic best, 8.72 m, to have a feel of the gold.

Fate, as though sympathetic that Carl has been unable to keep his promise, smiled at him. Three days after the 100m sprint, Ben Johnson, Carl's archrival, tested positive for steroid use. This led to his gold being stripped off and handed to Carl, who became the Olympic champion in the race.

Although the games ended with Carl making out with only two golds in the long jump and 100m race, a result he didn't expect, he was happy that his words to his mom, "Don't worry, I will get another one," wasn't in vain.

Offering his first Olympic gold to be buried with his father was the last homage he paid to the man who, together with his mom, Evelyn, introduced him to track and field events and was the major motivating force in his budding career.

Born into a middle-class family in Birmingham, Alabama, on July 1, 1961, and raised in the lively atmosphere of Willingboro, New Jersey, Carl and his siblings had a taste of childhood that gave them room to have choices.

Growing up, Carl and his siblings were exposed to the arts and sports. This allowed Carl to take dance, cello, and piano classes and attend plays and musicals. While this tickled his childhood fancies, it did not have enough grip to hold down his interest for a long while.

At 10, he found a new hobby when he started visiting the local athletics club run by his parents. The local athletics club did not just pleasure the young Carl; it birthed a spark in him, allowing him to challenge himself and push himself beyond his comfort zone. Competing with other young stars, who were also coached by his parents, in the local club birthed a passion for track and field events in Carl.

For a child not used to stretching and twisting his bones so much while growing up, his body needed to adjust to his newfound passion. It was a price his body had to pay.

So, at 15, he experienced he experienced a severe growth spurt that nearly crippled him. Having been considered too short for his age, his bones magically climbed up to two and a half inches in the space of a month. It was a painful experience that had him walk with crutches until his bones adjusted.

Willingboro High School saw a promising Carl run through its track and field events. Under the special guidance of coach Andy Dudek and Paul Minore, Carl was molded into one of the finest high school athletes in the country. He competed mainly in the long jump and set a new national prep record of 8.13 m (26ft-8in).

This earned him fourth place in the all-time World Junior list of long jumpers. His impressive records were a gravitational pull that dragged many colleges to him in 1979.

At 19, Carl knew exactly what he wanted to do with his life. Even with the mad scramble for him, he didn't want to sell himself short. He knew choosing the right college was crucial to early success in his career, which was something he wanted. This awareness made him take the hands of the University of Houston, Texas, where he thrived under Coach Tellez, who remained his coach until the end of his career.

However, Carl's careful assessment of his college options teaches the invaluable lesson that making important life choices is a serious business and must be treated as such.

True to his meticulous calculations, the University of Houston was his fastest track to an illustrious career. However, before his athleticism grew wings to fly in college, an old high school knee injury resurfaced with a bag of pains. Jumping became very traumatic, as each jump rattled his body with pain. With a bad knee that threatened his fitness, Carl was about to be pushed off quite early from the cliff of what would have been an impressive career. However, his coach, Tellez, knew his talent was not a gift one handed over to injury.

So, he introduced him to a new technique that helped him maintain his talent and knee injury. But the injury did not hold him back this time when he jumped. With a knee that posed no threats, Carl extended his athletic genius in the sprints.

He claimed his first-ever National Collegiate Athletic Association (NCAA) title. Stamping his name into NCAA history as the second person after Jesse Owens (who was his idol) to win the long jump and 100 meters at the college championship. With his impressive performance, making it to the American 1980 Olympic team was just a walk in the park.

However, his dream to break into the international scene during the 1980 Summer Olympics in Moscow, Russia, was cut short by the U.S. boycott of the games. But he soon realized that this was for the best after participating in the Liberty Bell Classic, where he won a bronze medal in the long jump and gold with the American team in the 4x100m relay.

Although this was an international event, he felt better that it was not the Olympics. Winning a medal in the Olympics would have dampened his spirit, but with this event, he knew he had a lot of work to do.

1981 saw a new 20-year-old, Carl, emerge in the athletic scene with a bag full of determination. It began with the Southwest Conference Championship in Dallas. Here Carl came with a bang, becoming the fastest sprinter in the world by finishing the 100 m race in a record time of 10 seconds. This was a quantum leap from his 1979 and 1980 finish times of 10.67 and 10.21 seconds, respectively.

At the end of the games, he had his first national titles in the long jump and 100-meter race in his pocket, which earned him the number one rank in both events. By the year's end, he claimed the James E. Sullivan Award as the top amateur athlete in the U.S.

This new win enlarged Carl's heart with a mountain of confidence that he would stand on throughout his career. From 1981 to 1992, Carl never loosened his grip on the 100-meter race and long jump. During this period, he ranked first in the race six times in all competitions and never went beyond third. In the long jump, his dominance saw him claim the number-one spot nine times before being ranked second in subsequent years.

Carl matched into the 1984 Olympics with a towering confidence. The echo of his dominance in the game was like the sun that no one could ignore. Having missed it four years ago due to the U.S. boycott, he wanted to announce his presence at the world's largest event in style.

One ambition burnt in his heart at the tournament: to match the landmark made by his idol, Jesse Owens, at the 1936 games in Berlin, where he won gold in four events. So, in Los Angeles, 1984, Carl entered the 100-meter race, long jump, 200-meter race, and 4x100 relay race and pocketed all golds.

One would expect that with the relative ease with which Carl had claimed the golds, companies would scramble to get him for endorsements. Carl had expected it, too, but it never really happened. This was primarily due to bad press, which framed the public's perception of him as arrogant and homosexual.

At the time, gay rights have not become a thing. So, his general non-macho appearance was a public turn-off. As a result of the rumors and the poor public image of his sexuality, he lost his contracts with Nike and Coca-Cola companies.

This was a tough time for Carl, but he did not crumble under the weight. He channeled his energy into his career. By the year's end, he held tightly to his number one world ranking spot in the 100-meter and long jump.

He mocked his detractors and claimed the number-one spot in the 200 m race. Finally, the Track and Field News named him the athlete of the year for the third time in a row. Carl's disposition throughout this turbulent time teaches one thing: the best revenge is always success.

Conscious of the media's dislike of his personality, he ensured he never starved them with his success story. With his continuous domination in track and field events, he became a mountain they could not push down but only hovered around it.

He turned the 1988 Olympic Games in Seoul, South Korea, the 1992 Games in Barcelona, Spain, and the Atlanta 1996 Games into a shopping mall he walked into with a shopping trolley, taking nine gold medals. He did the same in the World Championships, pocketing eight gold medals.

With an impressive record in track and field events sitting pretty in his name, in 1997, Carl decided to leave while the ovation was still high. Four years after he retired, at 40, Carl was inducted into the USA Track and Field Hall of Fame. This was followed by honors as an "Olympian of the Century" and "Sportsman of the Century" by Sports Illustrated and the International Olympic Committee, respectively.

Carl's story teaches the invaluable lesson that we must not depend on others' likes or dislikes to achieve success.

Speak your Mind

Have you ever had to change how you approach something to succeed, like studying differently for a tough subject, trying a new technique in sports, or finding a new strategy in a video game?

How do you think being versatile, like trying new approaches or learning new skills, can help you overcome challenges and succeed when things get tough?"

Overcoming Adversity with Versatility

Lewis faced significant challenges, including controversy over alleged drug use and intense competition. Despite this, he won nine Olympic gold medals across multiple events. Mental toughness includes adapting and succeeding in multiple disciplines, showing that versatility can be a strength.

NELLY KORDA

An unsettling feeling flushed down the faces of the spectators who gathered at the Sebonack Golf Club in Southampton, New York, to witness the 2013 68th U.S. Women's Open. A few moments ago, their faces were flush with excitement as they watched the jittery hands of amateur golfers making their first championship debut in the biggest prize in women's golf. However, it took the energetic hands of the tall, blonde 14-year-old Nelly, gripping her club with a firmness that stunned everyone, to snap them out of their excitement.

Nelly's daring confidence was not associated with amateur golfers debuting to make the Women's Open cut. The spectators were used to the puddle of sweat greasing the palms of the young golfers, the tickles of butterflies running wide in their tummy, and their evasion of the eyes of spectators that drilled fear into them. However, the aura that came with Nelly was not the regular. So, their curious eyes followed her like a shadow, watching her every movement.

Immediately, her club began gliding into the air with clinical precision; ready to take her first shot, one could see shock prying open the spectators' jaws, just wide enough to take in a golf ball.

Swoosh! She sent her first shot into flight. Their curious eyes chased after it. In seconds, their curious eyes moistened into cheerful smiles, and their hands became cymbals- clapping as Nelly's shot found the fairway. This was an impressive shot for a first-timer.

A pleasant surprise spread its hands wide on Nelly's face. The crinkles of smiles formed at the corners of her eyes showed that she hadn't expected much, given her general composure before her shot found the fairway. Speaking about her heroic first shot, she said, "It was nice; I didn't get nervous about the first hole, which was a big surprise. I just went up and hit it like a junior tournament,"

With Nelly's convincing shot, admiration took off the surprise that previously covered the faces of the spectators. So, when eventually, Nelly brilliantly finished with birdies on her last two holes, Nos. 8 and 9, it didn't come as a surprise. Although she made the U.S. Women's Open cut, shooting an impressive one over 73, which placed her seven points behind leader Ha-Neul Kim, the eventual winner of the Open, who had 66, Nelly carved a place in the hearts of the spectators who saw the talent in her and wanted to see her go pro.

Do you know the irony of the story? Nelly didn't come to the U.S. Open with high expectations of some of her peers who nursed the intention of going pro. She was just a teen having fun with a hobby she found interesting since childhood. The 2013 U.S. Women's Open was not different to her like the previous ones she'd been to.

However, the 2013 U.S. Women's Open struck a different chord in her heart. Perhaps it was because this time, instead of just watching like before, she played. The feeling struck a match of passion in her, which lit up an illustrious career that would place her number one in the world of women's golf.

She confirmed this years later when she said, "When I first played in the U.S. Women's Open, I was 14 years old, and walking on that range and seeing all the top names in women's golf and having my sister there and everything, I think that's where I fell in love with the game. I was like, 'Ok, this is what I want to do for the rest of my life.' That tournament would always be one of the most special that I will ever play in,"

Finding her passion in golf, Nelly pursued it with the urgency of one who had a deadline to catch. With parents who were pro tennis players (her father won the 1998 Australian Open), a pro tennis player brother, and a pro golfer sister, Nelly had not only sports running in her veins but also a good support system that inspired her and helped her gain clarity in her chosen profession. Hence, she began pedaling into an illustrious career that etched her name in gold.

Born on July 28, 1998, in Bradenton, Florida, in the cradle of a family whose bloodstream was injected with sports, Nelly's fingerprints carried the family trademark. Although her parents, Petre and Regina, were once professional tennis players, and his brother Sebastian queued in with them, she quickly queued in with her elder sister, Jessica, who took her under her wings in golf. For Nelly, at the time, golf was just a means of bonding with her big sister, who was about five years older. It didn't stop her from being interested in tennis and ice hockey.

So, at six, Nelly joined the family's sporting tradition by being trained at the nearby IMG Academy, where she had lessons about three to four times a week. Learning the trade of one of the most mentally and physically challenging sports was enough to sharpen her latent talent. Despite being a hobby for the young Nelly, she still worked hard for her dreams to come true.

With a budding talent that could not stay under the canopy of a mere hobby, Nelly was launched into a successful amateur career that took root after her successful run in the 2013 U.S. Women's Open. With a heart now burning with passion, evident in her statement, "I want to be the best golfer in the world. I want to be World No. 1, and I want to have the Grand Slam, and I want to work toward something that no one's ever done before,", Nelly went to work. Here, she leaves a lesson that success is not mere wishes.

Her hard work blossomed into early success during her amateur year in 2015. A year later, she had a magnet for hands and would pull in every laurel she came an inch close to. That year, she won the Harder Hall and PING Invitational, made the AJGA Rolex Junior All-American, and earned a place at the Junior Solheim Cup.

With an impressive season under her wing, which slowly spread her wings into the sky of the golf world, a war began to rage in the heart of the young star. It was her first major challenge.

Eighteen-year-old Nelly was torn between going to college to get a law degree or pursuing her passion, which had already picked momentum. Going to college would allow her to kill two birds with a stone: getting a degree in a traditional career path and the opportunity to play collegiate golf and make friends.

However, with a budding career on a winning streak, Nelly didn't consider a break in her momentum necessary. So, instead of going to college, she chose the shorter route to her dreams. With her decision, she saved the world of golf from a long wait for the arrival of a phenomenal star who would eventually turn around the world of women's golf.

The year 2016 sailed Nelly into the ocean of professional golf. With a bag full of extraordinary talent and determination, her career went live on the Symetra Tour. She came with the same confidence she had when she debuted at the 2013 U.S. Women's Open. However, this time, it was not the casual confidence of a carefree teenage girl who didn't bother about outcomes.

She came to the Symetra Tour in red-hot form. She clinched a win in her first professional tournament, the Sioux Falls Great Life Challenge, after a 3-stroke victory over Wichanee Meechai. This win was the scaffold she used to climb up the golf ladder. Her top 10 finish on the money list was her gate pass into the world of the Ladies Professional Golf Association (LPGA) in 2017.

Although her stay at the Symetra Tour was quite short, she left footprints by making statements about her aggression on the course, accurate iron play, powerful drives, and solid desire that didn't bow to pressure, which are trademarks of her impressive career. After breaking into the LPGA in 2017, she pocketed the Swinging Skirts LPGA Taiwan Championship, her first win in the LPGA that sent a clear signal that she had come for business.

After her first LPGA win, a certain reassured confidence sprouted in Nelly. The confidence came from the realization that she didn't make a mistake choosing golf. She was proud of herself. It was this confidence that launched her into a winning streak, and she never looked back.

In 2019, the 21-year-old Nelly walked to victory by winning the ISPS Handa Women's Australian Open. With this win, she moved from 16th place to 9th in the world Women's World Golf ranking, trailing behind Lexi Thompson to become the second-highest-ranked American in the golf world.

In 2021, Nelly officially decided to grab the pen of the history books of the women's golf world and spent the year writing only her name on it. It began on February 28 at Lake Nona Golf and Country Club in Orlando, Florida, where she won the Gain bridge LPGA. Three months after that, on June 20, she pocketed the Meijer LPGA Classic.

Without pausing to catch her breath, just seven days after that, on the 27th of June, in the final round of the KPMG Women's PGA Championship at the Atlanta Athletic Club, Nelly, with a 4-under 68 shots, won over Lizette Salas, this victory earned her first major. A major win pulled her from the number 9 in the world of women's golf and crowned her the number one.

One would think that with three wins already, she'd taken all she needed for the year. However, when a sunny day broke out on the 5th of August at the 2021 Summer Olympics in Japan, the 23-year-old Nelly showed the world that her tank was far from being filled.

In round 2 of the tournament, while anxiety made drumbeats with the racing heartbeats of the American fans, who had not claimed an Olympic gold medal in golf for over 121 years, Nelly's calm confidence did not let the fear pass through her. She needed to win, not just for America, but for herself.

Standing on the 18th tee at -11 for her round, with a firm grip on her club, she double-bogeyed the hole for a 62 and made history. She became the first

American woman to win gold in golf at the Olympics since 1900. A record that etched her name elegantly, both in history and in the hearts of Americans.

Barely two months after her historic win, Nelly, in November, pocketed her fourth LPGA victory of the year. She won the Pelican Women's Championship in Bellair, Florida, in a playoff over Lexi Thompson, Lydia Ko, and Kim Sei-young.

A loud feat that made her the first American since Stacy in the past eight years with four wins in the LPGA Tour Season. Her extraordinary run in 2021 made her a force of gravity in the world of golf. She went ahead to pull several wins and championships under her belt.

With the ease Nelly's wins keep flowing in droves, you'd be wrong to think she had claimed everything in the world of golf or had not suffered losses. Despite her career success, she has yet to pocket the one win she longed for throughout her career. The U.S. Women's Open. A win that has continually eluded the world champion. She nearly snatched a win at the event in 2018 and 2022, but 'nearly' never kills a bird.

The hopes of breaking the jinx rose to an all-time fever pitch high in the 2024 Women's Open when she walked into Lancaster Country Club. Having already walked her name once again into history books at the start of the year by winning five successive starts on the LPGA Tour, she was the favorite to win the 2024 Women's Open.

This time, even without her name boldly written on placards of fans at the Lancaster Country Club, cheering her to win, Nelly knew it was long overdue, and she needed to win. Her face was ripe with a red-hot desire to win.

If one had looked closely at her face as she was about to make her first shot, one would see something that had never appeared before, sitting gallantly on it. It was pressure and fear. Then it happened. In quick successions that left the once cheering crowd stunned. Her first three straight shots from inside, 70 feet away, found their way into a stream, forcing her to walk off the par-3 12th hole with a 10. The worst score she had ever gotten in her professional career.

The sheer unbelief of her disastrous start struck her. One could see how disappointment folded her head and crumbled her legs into a crouching position at the Lancaster Country Club. With a score like that, she had a slim chance of winning. Even with a slim chance, she didn't give up. However, another hard luck was nesting on the horizon. Sadly, her magnetic hands, once again, were too slippery to grab a cut in the U.S. Women's Open.

Disappointment replaced the sheen of excitement that was previously shunned in the eyes of the fans, who had gotten used to her winning everything and never thought she could lose. Nelly didn't let the loss bite into her confidence. She took her poor start in good fate.

When the press walked up to her, she didn't let sadness claim her voice. Speaking on her uneventful run, she said, "I am human. I'm going to have bad days. I played some good solid golf up to this point. Today was just a bad day. That's all I can say".

Although Nelly is still very active in the golf world and might eventually claim a win in the Women's Open, her story leaves invaluable lessons: We may not always get to win despite our best efforts. We will always win some and lose some. Losses always remind us that we are not some superhumans who get it every time. So, we must take it in good faith whenever we lose and try again.

Speak your Mind

Can you think of a time when you felt nervous or scared about doing something you love, like playing in a big soccer game, performing in a school play, or taking an important test?

Did knowing you worked hard help you overcome those feelings?

Overcoming Pressure and Fear through Passion and Hard Work

Overcoming pressure and fear through passion and hard work is essential for success. Take Nelly Korda's journey as an example. At just 14, Nelly competed in the U.S. Women's Open, a huge and intimidating event. Instead of being overwhelmed, her love for golf and her dedication to practice helped her stay calm and perform well.

She didn't give up even when she faced challenges and losses later in her career, like missing a cut at the U.S. Women's Open. She used her passion for the game and her commitment to hard work to keep improving. Remember, you can overcome any fear or pressure when you love something and work hard!

MICHAEL SCHUMACHER

Uncertainties trailed the 22-year-old Michael Schumacher like a shadow as he stepped into the cockpit of Jordan 191, poised to make his Formula One debut at the Belgian Grand Prix. Spa-Francorchamps Circuit was not a grid; any driver with no experience wakes up and decides to drive on because of its twists and turns. However, Michael was to be an exception. The Jordan team contracted him at the very last minute to replace the team's champ, Bertrand Gachot, who was arrested for an assault.

A heavy cloud of obvious questions gathered in the eyes of Jordan's team fans. There were doubts if the little-known Michael could fit into the large shoes of Gachot because until Michael walked behind the wheel of Jordan 191, he was just a driver under Formula 3, with cars far below the Formula One car.

Even with his face tucked into Jordan's racing helmet, Michael could see the unsheathed swords of unbelief Jordan's team fans eyes wielded thrusting into him. In his calm demeanor, he didn't seem bothered. Why would he be worried? When his whole life up till that moment has been a long winding track that had nothing running on it but the tires of his passion.

Born on January 3rd, 1969, in Hurth-Hermulhein, West Germany, to a bricklayer father who managed the local karting track in his hometown, Kerpen, and a mother who ran a canteen there, Michael's first playground was automatically the karting track. Even in young Michael's childish babblings, his father could see his boy's interest in karting. So, he did what every good parent would have done to nurture his interest.

At the age of four, Michael began karting with a homemade pedal kart his father made for him. Watching his son master the pedal kart, he fitted a small motorcycle engine to the kart. Michael struggled to master the new upgrade. A crash into a lamppost, rather than sprinkling dust of fear into his eyes, gave him his first lesson on the risky nature of the profession his young mind was pining for. This lesson made him into a meticulous driver, which he later became. Michael had mastered his new machine by age six and was ready to compete.

However, Michael's dream was a mountain the budget of his low-income family could not climb. This nearly robbed the world of motorsport, one of its finest drivers. His parents' faith saved his dreams.

Believing in their son's dream and willing to support him in the best way they could, they began to reach out to local businessmen in their community who were enthusiasts of the sport for sponsorships. This was the light that shunned into Michael's darkness.

Michael, for his part, knew the challenges that faced him like the back of his palm. So, he put his best foot forward, knowing that first impressions may not give room for second chances. He officially began to race competitively after getting his license at age 12. From 1984 to 1987, he pocketed the German and European Kart Championships.

Michael's head was trapped in a noose again when the sponsorships his parents rallied stopped coming. This, thankfully, did not take away Michael's fire. With a mind that burnt with the fuel of pure passion and an untiring quest for improvement, he continued to improve himself.

Michael left school to help support his family and devote more time to his craft. He began working as an apprentice car mechanic, an experience that molded him into a mechanically aware driver, giving him an edge over his peers.

At 19, the stars began to align in Michael's favor during his stint as a mechanic. He got a chance as a race driver for the Mercedes sports car team in the German Formula Three (F3) car series. Although the F1 series was low-ranked, for someone like Michael, who had spent most of his life making lemonades out of bitter lemon, he knew he must make the best of the opportunity.

In 1990, two years after joining the series, his breakthrough came. He won the F3 Championship title, which sent ripples of sensation across the vast ocean of Formula 3. His incredible talent, speed, and work ethic made him a star in a dark cloud, brimming radiantly for everyone to see. His star brought him luck in an unexpected turn of events: the arrest of Formula One's champion, Bertrand Gachot. A search for a replacement began afterward.

The result of this search got him seated behind the wheel of Jordan 191 in 1991, at the beginning of this story, with the doubtful eyes of the teams' fans pouring on him like floodlights. Driving in the highly ranked Formula One Series was his leverage to climb the race ladder.

So, Michael kept his bespectacled eyes on the track, ready to step on the throttle. This was his chance, and he was going to take it. Once the race began, the curious eyes of the fans chased after him. A few meters into the unfamiliar grid, the 22-year-old Michael bullied his way into the eighth place.

Warmth began to break the ice of doubts nesting on the fans' faces. However, it seemed the Jordan 191 wheel just wanted to give the fans a taste of Michael's potential. Once it got their attention, barely moments into the race, its clutch failed, denying the fans the feel of what could have been. Though short, his impressive 7th-place finish sent a signal into the F1 world. This marked the beginning of one of the most accomplished world drivers in Formula One.

The clutch failure brought his contract with the Jordan team to a hurried end. With an impressive record in his pocket already, he was signed by the Benetton team in 1992. By joining the Mercedes Junior Racing Programme, opportunities knocked at his door. He had the opportunity to compete in the World Endurance Championship. With his skillful hands behind the Sauber-Mercedes C291, he won races in Mexico City and Autopolis.

After claiming successful wins in the early 90s in races such as the Japanese 300 Championship and the German Touring Car Championship, between 1994 and 1995, he won the Drivers World Championship. Although Michael's name had become a sensation that burnt on everyone's tongue, the end of the 1995 season marked the beginning of his first major challenge in his profession.

Michael decided to join the Italian Ferrari team. This decision sent many tongues wagging. Many of his fans didn't consider it a good move. Given his impressive records at Benetton, they thought a move to Ferrari would cripple the wings of his career that just took off.

However, Michael showed enormous mental strength by not bowing to pressure to reconsider his decision. In 1996, he went ahead to join the Italian team Ferrari, which had not won a Driver's championship title since 1979. Trusting his guts, Michael joined the team and made it his home.

Michael's decision at this point in his career teaches us that we must build enough mental strength in the journey toward success. Because we will have to make tough decisions that may not sit well with everyone, we must trust our guts and do what feels true without bowing to outside pressures.

Coming into the team, Michael didn't expect what would turn out to be a year's run to be a walk in the park. So, he came with a backpack full of incredible work ethic, infectious optimism, and high energy.

In his first season with the Ferrari team, he finished third in the championship. Of course, he wasn't expecting to finish first at this point. It was not going to be an easy run, remember? He kept working hard through the years and waited for a breakthrough.

The opportunity came in 1999 during the British Grand Prix at Silverstone. Michael walked into the eighth round of the FIA Formula One World Championship with a tall ambition. The Ferrari team has yet to win a title in 20 years. The championship was a perfect opportunity to break the jinx. Lined up in the front row and seated in his Ferrari399, just behind his archrival Hakkinenen, Michael's face held a cold grimace that didn't breathe a smile. It seemed the weight of his ambition weighed on him.

With the billowing wind hovering, it seemed it would be a bad race for Michael. After a few laps on the drags, he was handed a relegation that took him from the second to the fourth place behind McLaren of David Coulthard. This was a hard hit on Michael's chances.

Determined to regain his position and take the lead, he pressed down on his throttle with the impatience of one with a lot at stake. He breezed through challenging corners at the Silverstone Circuit—Maggots, Becketts, and Chapel Complex. These sections are known for their high-speed demands and intricate curves. Michael's skillful move through these corners ushered him into the slipstream leading straight to the Hangar Straight.

A look ahead reveals two officers waving red flags, signaling the race to a momentary stop. There had been a stall in the grid due to Villeneuve's scar, which was stuck in gear and on the racing line. While other drivers who acknowledged the raced flags stopped, Michael and his teammate, fully immersed in the race, missed it and kept racing towards the Stowe corner. With Michael already inside the line, desperately edging for an overtake to reclaim his place, he saw the car stuck in gear on the racing, but it was too late.

Tragedy struck! His break failed. In split seconds, he quickly flew towards the tire barriers. The heavy impact swallowed the noise of the crowd and left fallen looks on the faces of the Ferrari team. Michael's machine was a total wreck, and he was trapped in it. Seeing his hope slipping off his hands, the visibly frustrated Michael made a desperate attempt to get out of the wreck. It held onto him like a leech until the marshalls rushed to the scene to steal him from it.

With a broken right leg and a sprinkle of bruises, Michael's title run screeched to a premature end. This was the most fatal accident of his career. But for someone who began crashing into Lampposts at a tender age, an accident wasn't something he had to bat an eyelid for. The accident turned out to be the last crow before daybreak. It marked a turning point in his career. Instead of pushing him to find another team, it unleashed an iron will and a fighting spirit that molded him into a monster behind the wheel.

When he bounced back in 2000, as though in a quest to avenge himself, the Championship was the first thing the 31-year-old Michael laid his hands on. A win that gave the Ferrari team their first driver's title in twenty years. His grip held on tightly to the title from 2000 to 2004. He turned the sport into a personal playing ground, pocketing everything on his way.

By the time he retired in 2006 at the age of 37, he had successfully claimed 91 Grand Prix wins, 77 fastest laps, and 68 pole positions. He also broke an almost 50-year record by winning 7 Drivers World Championships (previously held by Juan Manuel, who had just five).

Like every true athlete, Michael decided to bow out when the ovation was still high. He finished his mind-blowing career with the Italian Ferrari team. Before he drew the curtain, he had made history in his Ferrari team, which he fondly refers to as family. He led the team to six consecutive Constructors Championships and won all of them. But apart from his unrivaled success in the team, the one thing one can never miss was the mutual love their hearts bore for each other.

During his tenure on the team, he was considered the most hardworking driver. This was not just due to the way he drove the team to success but also due to the way he related to everyone: his co-drivers, factory workers, and other personnel. He was always found, never judging or criticizing; instead, he encouraged and inspired everyone with his contagious energy.

These gestures burnt him into their heart. So, after his retirement, the team kept him close by employing him as their test driver and adviser. The lesson here for everyone to pick is the need to build good working relationships and give our best wherever we find ourselves.

Michael made headlines in 2009 when he announced that he would be returning to the sport he retired from barely three years ago. This news, like his decision to join Ferrari about fourteen years ago, was met with backlash and concerns from the public and his fans. They did not see the point of returning to a sport where he had given sweat and blood to take everything that needed taking. They feared he would ruin his impressive record with that decision.

However, Michael did not set his shoulders to bear the burden of pressure. Many suggested that the decision was due to his long-standing relationship with Ross Brawn, who worked as a technical director in the Ferrari team throughout his career. Brawn was to head the new Formula One Mercedes team. Michael, pulled by friendship and curiosity, joined the team in 2010 amidst backlash.

The public's predictions seem to be right this time around. Although he gave his best in his three seasons with the team, old age and the army of new world champions who were almost a decade younger kept his hand away from every title. He didn't win a race in his three-year stint and was not placed higher than eight in the F1 standing.

Finally, conscious that age has come upon him, he decided to call it quits. His uneventful run in the three years seems to be a kind of experiment for him. His face didn't carry the scar of one who lost for three seasons. While speaking to the press with the sheer avuncularity of one who didn't take his uneventful run to heart, he said, "I enjoyed most of it. It wasn't successful as before, but I still learned a lot about life. I found that losing can be both more difficult and more instructive than winning. Now, is a good time to go".

Speak your Mind

Can you think of a time when you spent more time on something, like practicing a sport, learning a new skill, or completing a school project?

How did your commitment and effort make a difference in how things turned out? Do you think the same kind of hard work and dedication could help you achieve bigger goals, like becoming great at a sport or getting good grades?

Hard Work and Commitment

To stay committed to your passion, remember that dedication is key to success. Michael Schumacher, one of the greatest Formula 1 drivers, didn't become a champion overnight. He practiced relentlessly, stayed focused on his goals, and never gave up, even when faced with challenges.

Here are some tips to help you stay committed:

- **Set Clear Goals:** Know what you want to achieve and break it down into smaller steps.
- **Practice creatively:** Think of a new and fun way to practice your passion daily so you won't get bored.
- **Stay Positive:** Believe in yourself, even when things get tough.
- **Learn from Mistakes:** Every mistake is a chance to improve. Don't give up!

Printed in Great Britain
by Amazon

48230190R00069